Praise FOR
STUBBORN *Obedience*

"Stubborn Obedience reminds us that God is after our faithfulness, even though we're all flawed. God graciously empowers us for the obedience He calls us to. A very helpful book."

– Dr. Ed Litton, Pastor of Redemption
Church in Mobile, AL

"What an incredible story of God's unexpected but perfect plan! This book is a powerful encouragement to families everywhere that are walking a 'by faith' journey. Holly delivers this charming and encouraging recount with wit and honesty. This book feels like a conversation over a cup of coffee at the kitchen table - full of love, laughter, and inspiration!"

– Charity Gayle, songwriter and Gospel
Music recording artist

"Ever struggle to understand what the Lord is telling you to do? At times the Lord calls us to do things that make no sense and often seem impossible. Moving forward in your faith journey will take courage, tenacity and perhaps stubborn obedience. Holly Knight's story is raw and real and highlights God's faithfulness in the life of a family who heard God speak."

– Debbie Stuart, Women's Minister at
Green Acres Baptist Church in Tyler, TX,
and author of Redeemed Rebel

"When I read Stubborn Obedience, not only did it resonate with the faithfulness of God I had seen in Holly's life, it stirred a work of faith in me, and encouraged me in ways I didn't even expect. I can't imagine anyone reading this God-honoring offering and not being compelled to love, trust and serve Christ in deeper ways."

- TRAVIS COTTRELL, WORSHIP PASTOR AT BRENTWOOD BAPTIST CHURCH IN BRENTWOOD, TN, AND WORSHIP LEADER FOR LIVING PROOF LIVE WITH BETH MOORE

"With brutal honesty, Holly Knight skillfully illustrates how God uses our stubborn obedience to accomplish great things in our lives. An encouraging, inspiring read."

- KATHY FERGUSON LITTON, NORTH AMERICAN MISSION BOARD

"Holly Knight is as real as it gets. She has a personality that energizes the entire room, a sense of humor that will leave you rolling on the floor, and a faith that is as bold as a Texas sunset. Her book, Stubborn Obedience, is no different. You will leave these pages encouraged, inspired, and deeply motivated to run harder after Jesus. Leaving no stone unturned, Holly authentically shares the ups and downs (and ins and outs) of her adoption journey while pointing to God's faithfulness the entire way. If you have any doubt that God will show up for you, this is the book for you. It is a bold reminder to us of all that God can do when we walk in obedience (even if it's stubborn)."

- BECKY LEACH, ARTIST, AUTHOR OF THE PIVOT, AND FOUNDER OF FREETOOTX

"Holly Knight is a dear friend. I knew it would be easy to write something good about this incredible "light". She shines in every room she enters. But I was stunned by the depth of her faith and confidence as I started reading the details of her journey. I knew 'in part' about the obstacles she faced as she traveled to Africa to begin the process of adopting two precious children, James and Jolie, whom I have come to adore. But as I began reading the first few paragraphs of this amazing story, I was completely pulled in and could not put the book down. Holly's ability to paint a picture on the canvas of our imaginations is absolutely stunning. This story is breathtaking. Get ready for an amazing journey. Once you begin, you're not going to be able to stop reading."

- DAVID BINION, PASTOR OF DWELL CHURCH IN ALLEN, TX, SONGWRITER, AND AUTHOR OF THE INVISIBLE WORSHIPER

"Holly Knight is a gifted writer - you can see her personality come through every page. She is funny, straightforward, and encouraging; and her writing speaks straight to my soul. I have firsthand knowledge to her story, and I am still amazed at all she's walked through. You'll be totally drawn in by Holly's quick wit and authenticity. She never holds back truth, and her vulnerability is refreshing. I'm so excited to see what God will do through her family's story."

- ANGIE BROWN, WOMEN'S PASTOR AT NINETEEN:TEN CHURCH IN BOERNE, TX

"I've known Holly almost twenty years and, after reading this book, readers will feel they know her, too. Holly leaves nothing on the table when describing the journey God called her family to travel. Readers will relate to her emotion, hesitation and questions, but will ultimately be encouraged and challenged by her willingness to step out in faith and walk in obedience. Holly shares the incredible and harrowing story of bringing her Ugandan children home, and throughout it all she points to our big God who went before her, walked beside her, and guides her still today. This is a must-read for anyone needing encouragement and confidence to walk in faith."

- TASHA CALVERT, GLOBAL WOMEN'S MINISTER
AT PRESTONWOOD CHURCH IN PLANO, TX

"My years-long friendship with Holly Knight has brought much joy to my life. To read the words she has poured out for us here in her story of obedience has me, first of all, laughing as only Holly can do! And at the same time, crying big crocodile tears as I contemplate what it looks like to lay our lives down before the Lord; to know the privilege of partnering with Him in accomplishing His will in the earth. What does that look like in my life? In your life? As you take in Holly's story of Stubborn Obedience, the Lord will speak deeply to you and you'll come to know the joy of following Christ in a much greater way."

- NICOLE BINION, PASTOR OF DWELL CHURCH
IN ALLEN, TX, GOSPEL MUSIC RECORDING
ARTIST

"In high-definition, Holly Knight elegantly and humorously captures what it looks like to walk by faith in the real world. Stubborn Obedience articulates the natural that elevates the supernatural. You are gonna learn something really special. And you are going to enjoy reading it while you do."

- AMIE DOCKERY, LEAD PASTOR OF COVENANT
CHURCH IN CARROLLTON, TX, AND AUTHOR OF
UNFOLLOW YOUR HEART AND DESIGNING YOUR
DREAM HUSBAND

"Unless I knew better, I would have never guessed in a million years this was Holly Knight's first stab at publishing. She's an engaging and inspiring writer. Her account of God's faithfulness in Stubborn Obedience is riveting and emotional. Her ability to tell God's story while using His word to teach us, the reader, feels part joy ride and part Bible Study. Holly is relatable, humble, and really funny. Having walked this journey with her, I know the roller coaster of emotions her obedience took her on. It was a long ride, full of ups and downs and twists and turns, and she recounts every single step with authenticity and accountability. If you've ever struggled with God's call on your life, you'll find the Knight's story in Stubborn Obedience encouraging and compelling."

- LISA CLARK, AUTHOR OF RAISING SINNERS, HOST OF THE WONDER PODCAST, RAISING SINNERS PODCAST, AND THE CHRISTIAN PARENTING PODCAST NETWORK

"Bigger than life! Excruciatingly honest. You never know what Holly will say next, yet she says what so many people are thinking. Then she goes further than that – with her huge heart for God, she frames her words in Biblical examples that help shine light on all our lives. It is my absolute delight to watch God's incredible plan unfold in Holly's life."

- BEVERLEY SUMRALL, PASTOR OF CATHEDRAL OF PRAISE IN MANILA, PHILIPPINES

"With great transparency and empathy, Holly Knight reminded me of my anointing and calling. Her word-smithing is impeccable… enough to keep this old athlete's attention. I laughed out loud, cried for breakthrough, and "amened" through the entire book. Holly's heart is put on full display in Stubborn Obedience."

- JASON BROWN, PASTOR OF NINETEEN:TEN CHURCH IN BOERNE, TX

STUBBORN OBEDIENCE

STUBBORN
Obedience

DISCOVER GOD'S RELENTLESS
FAITHFULNESS THROUGH
STEADFAST SURRENDER.

HOLLY KNIGHT

All Scripture quotations, unless otherwise indicated, are taken from the
CSB® Bible (The Holy Bible, Christian Standard Version®),
Copyright © 2017 by Holman Bible Publishers.

To Ava, Greta, Harper, James, and Jolie –
This story belongs to all of us.
The 5 of you are my greatest adventure.

TABLE OF *Contents*

Foreword

Once upon a time a sweet, beautiful and Jesus-loving couple got married. They stood in a church and said their vows in front of God, friends and family. But on that day, God, in His infinite wisdom, saw through the years and rested His gaze on two little brown babies in Africa. Standing between that young couple and these two babies were years of character building, years of learning to say yes to God, and years of allowing Him to determine their steps.

I remember the first time I met Holly Knight. We were attending a conference for Worship Pastors called Metro, and it was hosted by her church in the North Dallas area. I don't remember much about that conversation except that we were walking down a long foyer and she told me she was about to adopt two children from Uganda.

"Wow. That's hard." I felt it in my gut.

I remember being inspired by her willingness to go through such a rigorous process in a foreign country – all the way on the other side of the world. I had friends who had adopted domestically and saw the their steadfast determination. I knew it was hard.

Everyone who meets Holly instantly likes her. I knew Holly from afar for years. Our husbands were friends and had probably worked together at some point, but once I actually met Holly, we connected on Facebook. I began following her posts about the pending adoption. Then, as she and Bradley made their way to Uganda, I followed her updates with an urgency I can't explain. I remember worrying that I had missed an update, and even changing her setting in my Facebook feed to "favorites", so I wouldn't miss a single update. I was all in with this adoption. I was invested.

I was invested for a few reasons, one of them being I, too, was adopted as a baby. I was brought home from the hospital by a family I was not born into, but was adopted into as a chosen daughter. As I followed Holly's story, I connected with those little Ugandan babies half-way across the world. They would be leaving what was familiar and confronted by a new way of life. I knew they would eventually have questions. I knew they would eventually feel a disconnect. I knew they would let their minds wonder one day about what could've been. But I also knew that eventually they would realize that as adoptees, we have been given a gift that not all Christ-followers have. We have a unique perspective on the heart of our Heavenly Father. You see, even though I was born a little fair-skinned, red-headed girl in a hospital in Memphis, Tennessee, James and Jolie's story is my story. But it's not only my story. If you are a follower of Jesus, it's your story as well. Our God is a Good Father who "sets the orphan in families." [Psalm 68:6] We have all been adopted and chosen into His family.

Wouldn't it be great to be part of the Knight family – Christ-filled, beautiful, talented and just plain fun? How much more wonderful is it to be adopted into the family of God – to be called and chosen before the foundations of the world? We are chosen not based on our own merit, but on the gift of Jesus' obedience to graft us into His family.

As I read about Holly's stubborn obedience, I kept thinking of the unstoppable force behind her surrender. It's a force so strong and so powerful, that when met with immovable objects, the obedience persisted and prevailed. That force inside Holly is nothing short of the Holy Spirit. What happens when an unstoppable force meets an immovable object? Stones are rolled away and what was once dead comes back to life. Can I get an Amen? Holly was met with multiple immovable objects in the form of government officials, passports, red tape and visas. But the power of the Holy Spirit and the calling of God on her life were the unstoppable forces that led to accomplishing the impossible. Just as Jesus set His face like flint in determined resolution to go to the cross so we could be called children of God, so should we do likewise when God calls us. Obedience isn't always easy. In fact it almost never is. But the reward is immeasurably satisfying. As Holly writes, "Peace is the by-product of obedience." As you read these words, may you find that unstoppable force of stubborn obedience inside you to do exactly what He is calling you to do today.

"Yes." It's a simple three-letter word that often comes with some not-so simple consequences. I cannot think of a better person to tell the story of Stubborn Obedience than my friend, Holly. She handles the history of her children with such care, and she has invited us into a very sacred and holy space with her and her family. I hope you will cherish this gift you've been given in the words of this book. Embrace them. Enjoy them. Remember them. The words you're about to read are such a good gift.

ANGIE ELKINS
OWNER OF ANGIE ELKINS MEDIA,
DIRECTOR OF PODCASTS FOR JAMIE IVEY

Introduction

Hey, Friend. (Yes, we are already friends. Trust me on this one.) I can't believe you're holding a copy of this book. It's my very first book and it's been 9 years in the making. I've known that I was supposed to write this story for quite a while, but I ran from it like Usain Bolt. Writing a book was at the very top of my list of Things I Never Want To Do. Why? Because I'm tired. I'm a Mom of 5 kids. My time is not my own. I don't go to the bathroom by myself. I'm lucky if I get to take a shower more than once a week. *Hygiene?* Never heard of her. Laundry is my nemesis. I can clean my house and it will stay that way for exactly 23.5 minutes until my tornado children blow through and demolish everything in sight. As you can probably imagine, sitting down and writing a whole book sounded like the absolute worst thing I could ever do. But, good grief, God was persistent with me. And outrageously patient. He wouldn't let me off the hook. I've known that my family's story was meant to bless people. I knew I had to sit down and write it out myself; with my words, in my voice. And now you hold it in your hands. But before we go any further, I need to establish some ground rules, so we're on the same page.

This is not a book about adoption. In the coming chapters, you'll read the narrative of my family's journey with adoption. I'm going to take you through the entire timeline; from hearing the call of God, to bringing 2 babies home from Africa. You'll get the full story. What you won't find in this book? Answers regarding *should* you adopt, or *how* to adopt. There are many reasons for this, the main one being *I am not an adoption expert.* I'm nearly a decade into this thing, and I still have so much to learn. Adoption is nebulous, nuanced, difficult, beautiful Kingdom work. If you feel as if God is calling you into this world, I encourage you to research some local ministries or adoption support groups in your area and get plugged in. I've added a short list of helpful resources in the Appendix based off of my limited knowledge and experience. I'm praying that God gives you clarity and direction as you pray through this heavy assignment.

This book is just as much about you as it is about me. I couldn't fill an entire book with sentences just about me and my family. We're not that interesting. In almost every chapter, you'll read a portion of my story and find out how it applies to you, right where you are today. You'll (hopefully) be inspired to believe God and follow Him in total surrender with whatever task He's assigned to you. You'll discover God's unwavering faithfulness to those He calls. You'll get to decide if stubborn obedience is worth it.

So sit back and settle in. Grab a cup of coffee and some snacks. Or a Chick-fil-A tea. (I like mine unsweetened with 2 Stevia.) Turn the baby monitor off (your baby will be fine), send your kids outside to play (and tell them to stay there until the sun goes down, for the love), go hide behind your mountain of dirty laundry (it doesn't smell that bad), and buckle your seatbelt. We're going on a wild ride together. Just me and you. Two new friends.

♡ Holly

chapter 1

SHE HAS *Potential*

I don't like kids.

Being a mother was never on my radar. I envisioned motherhood as constant exhaustion and chaos, thanklessly chasing around ill-mannered, snot-nosed, dirty-diapered children. I think my disdain for children originated because, as a minister's daughter, I was the go-to babysitter for every young family in our congregation; and because my family was in "ministry," getting paid a decent wage to keep precious demon offspring alive and well-fed was a pipe dream. The PTSD I still have from babysitting two particular little beasts for six straight hours only to be handed a $10 bill at the end of the day is still fresh, almost 25 years later. It's no wonder that becoming a mother was never a fantasy of mine.

I had dreams. I had aspirations. I had arena tours to sell out and platinum-selling albums to record. There were countless radio and television interviews awaiting me and pristinely choreographed music videos to release. I was too fabulous for motherhood. So, the fact that I got married at 19 and became the mom of five children by the age of 29 should confirm the following:

- There is a God in heaven with a great sense of humor.
- God's plans for our lives often have little to do with us, and more to do with those He chooses to redeem through our obedience.
- God delights in accomplishing impossible things through stubborn, hard-headed, broken people like me.

I could end the book right now and give an altar call, but of course, I won't. I have a story to tell.

THREE LITTLE WORDS

Let's take a trip back to the 90's, when music was music, the glory days of land lines, Number 2 pencils, CD's, disposable cameras, Blockbuster Video, Reading Rainbow—before the world went mad with the venomous infiltration of the world wide web and social media. My childhood was enchanted. Growing up in the beautiful state of Colorado, I had the Rocky Mountains as my playground. My father was a worship pastor and an avid fly fisherman. We spent countless Fridays crammed into our cherry red Chevy truck, meandering up I-70 to some new campground near a mosquito-laden, fish-filled river. Our trusty pop-up camper trailer was clamped tightly to the hitch behind us.

My mother was the music teacher at the Christian school my siblings and I attended. There, I established deep, healthy friendships that have stayed with me to this day. At both my church and school, I developed a passion for singing and quickly discovered my life's calling was to lead others into the presence of the Lord. I was naturally gifted at communicating through song and felt most alive while leading people in a corporate setting. I had grand plans for my life as the next Grammy Award-winning diva of the Contemporary Christian Music scene. The only thing bigger than my personality was my self-confidence.

My parents raised me to be a leader. My father, who is now in heaven with Jesus, was my champion. He believed in me. He was my biggest encourager and loudest cheerleader. He pushed me to be better in every endeavor. He was always truthful about my faults and where I could improve. He was incredibly measured, grounded, and wise. Once, while speaking to a friend about me, I overheard him say something that left a permanent mark and will stay with me forever:

"She has potential."

As a mother now, I know the intention behind his words was to praise me and admonish me to his friend. But in that moment, at the impressionable age of 18, I assigned my own interpretation to those three words. In my mind, I assumed to know exactly what he meant. I immediately pinned my highest hopes and deepest fears about myself to that single phrase. The ultimate double-edged compliment and criticism: She has potential.

I have potential!

… to rule the world, to chase all my dreams and catch them, to be amazing at whatever I decide to do, to shine brightly, to illuminate the darkness, to win every race, to be used mightily by the Lord to further His kingdom, to change the world, to be wildly successful. Yes, I have potential!

Ah, but I also have potential.

… to open my big fat mouth and ruin everything, to say the wrong thing to the wrong person at the wrong time, to cross the invisible line into the inappropriate, to embarrass everybody within arm's reach, to untether my tongue, to be stupid, to flop, to fail miserably.

Yes, I have potential.

I have potential for absolute greatness, and potential for catastrophic disaster. That's me in a nutshell. I've spent most of my adult life straddling the line of my potential. Am I going to excel and win and thrive? Or am I going to crash and burn and fall flat on my face? It feels like a constant toss-up.

I would imagine that you, Friend, sometimes feel the same. You are keenly aware of your fallibility and fragility, knowing you could lose your marbles at any moment. You measure your lack of ability and qualifications against the scale of every big decision or every great calling that seems to loom over you. You know you could mess everything up in the blink of an eye. We all feel it. Because we're all human.

GOOD COMPANY

Do you know who else grappled with the possibility of epic failure? Literally everyone in the Bible other than Jesus. Seriously. Open the Scriptures to any random page and you'll find the story of a man or a woman (or a nation or a church) wrestling with the trappings of their humanity. This is a tale as old as time. So I guess you and I are in good company.

Let's hop over to the Old Testament and look at the legendary life of David: the shepherd boy turned monarch. He was selected as king over Israel at an early age. Set apart, ordained, called for the Lord's specific purpose. The prophet Samuel anointed David in the presence of his brothers, "and the Spirit of the Lord came powerfully on him from that day forward." [i] David went on to kill the giant Goliath and defeat the entire Philistine army. He led the Israelites into numerous battles and defeated every foe. The Lord established a covenant with David as king and promised to bless him and his descendants. David led the nation of Israel into a season of great prosperity. In other words, David lived up to his full potential.

But dang, David also failed miserably. The great favor of God over his life was at times eclipsed by even greater fiascos. Much of his life was an utter wreck of carnage brought about by his own doing. For instance, David got a little too cocky and decided to hang out at the palace while his men were off to war. He saw a naked woman bathing on her rooftop and instead of doing the right thing and looking away, he lusted after her and used his position as king to seduce her into an adulterous affair. The bathing beauty got pregnant and eventually gave birth to a son who died. Rather than immediately repenting and seeking forgiveness, David decided to have the lady's husband put on the front lines of battle, ensuring his death. So now, our hero is a murderer. Oh, and David's other son committed incest with his sister and is then murdered by his brother. (Kinda makes your

---

i   1 Samuel 16:13

family's Thanksgiving dinner squabbles feel like child's play, doesn't it?) The end of David's reign as king was marked by a plague that killed 70,000 men. Have I painted a sordid enough picture of the monumental failure that was David's life?

Except David's life wasn't a monumental failure. His life was marked by what could possibly be the greatest superlative of all time: *David was a man after God's own heart.*[ii] I've heard this a thousand times, but it never ceases to blow my mind. How could David, with all his faults and flaws, with all his sins and shortcomings, be considered a man after God's own heart?

The answer is simple: David was tenacious enough to believe in the faithfulness of the God who called him. David was headstrong in his reliance on the unchanging covenant God had established with him. David was steadfast in his worship and adoration of the God who chose him, in spite of all his blunders. David was stubborn.

I want to be like David. Don't you?

David lived in total dependence on the Lord. He was a shepherd, the least of his brothers. A total nobody. So much so, his father Jesse didn't even ask him to come in from tending the sheep to be presented to the prophet Samuel as a candidate for king. He was passed over and overlooked. But God saw him. And God chose him to fulfill a great purpose on this earth and to enter into an unbreakable covenant. David was not qualified. But David was anointed. And David chose to believe God.

I want my words to echo David's:

Make your ways known to me, Lord;

---

ii   1 Samuel 13:14

teach me your paths.
Guide me in your truth and teach me,
for you are the God of my salvation;
I wait for you all day long.
Remember, Lord, your compassion
and your faithful love,
for they have existed from everlasting.
Do not remember the sins of my youth
or my acts of rebellion;
in keeping with your faithful love,
remember me
because of your goodness, Lord.
The Lord is good and upright;
therefore he shows sinners the way.
All the Lord's ways show faithful love
and truth
to those who keep his covenant
and decrees.
Lord, for the sake of your name,
forgive my iniquity, for it is immense.
(Psalm 25:4-11)

Do you see the source of David's confidence in these verses? It's not in his own great potential, abilities, or accolades. David's confidence is in the goodness of God. His reliance was rooted in the fact God cannot break a promise or denounce His nature. God is faithful, upright, true, full of compassion. God is love. And God cannot go against His character. He's stubborn like that.

TOO MUCH FOR ME TO HANDLE

In the upcoming chapters of this book, you're going to read the story of how God called me—a nobody—to fulfill a great assignment. God didn't call me because I'm awesome. He didn't choose me because of my great potential, abilities, or accolades. In fact, I believe the opposite is true.

God called me because He's awesome and I was 100% unqualified.

And isn't that like God? He uses the foolish things to confound the wise. He uses the weak to shame the strong.[iii] In fact, the Lord tells Paul, "My power is perfected in weakness," to which Paul responds:

> Therefore, I will most gladly boast all the more about my weaknesses, so that Christ's power may reside in me. So I take pleasure in weaknesses, insults, hardships, persecutions, and in difficulties, for the sake of Christ. For when I am weak, then I am strong.
> (2 Corinthians 12:9-10)

So we shouldn't be surprised when the task at hand is too much for us to handle. It was always supposed to be too much for us to handle. It's in total surrender to God that His power is perfected in us, and we conquer the thing.

What has God called you to do, Friend? What has He put in you to accomplish that is a million times bigger than you could imagine? What assignment is in front of you that scares

iii   1 Corinthians 1:27

the living daylights out of you and makes you break out in a cold sweat? What dream has God given you that seems impossible? We serve a God who delights in the impossible. It's time to stop second-guessing your calling and stressing out about your potential to fail miserably. It's time to fix your eyes on the God who called you, who takes great joy in fulfilling His promises. It's time to believe that "He who calls you is faithful; he will surely do it."[iv]

Friend, it's time to believe God. Just like King David, it's time to stubbornly believe in the Almighty God who has been stubbornly faithful to you.

---

iv 1 Thessalonians 5:24

chapter 2

BABY *Boom*

Buckle up, and let's make a return trip back to the dawn of the new millennium: the year 2000. *NSync was tearin' up our hearts and the Backstreet Boys wanted it that way. (*NSync forever. I will fight you over this.)

I was living my best life as a senior in high school. The world was my bedazzled oyster. I had a major decision to make: pursue a potential record deal or take the vocal scholarship that was offered to me at a Christian university. I was leaning toward the record deal. (Remember: world tour, TRL, music videos?) My dad was leaning toward the scholarship. (Remember: measured, grounded, wise?) God was kicked back on His throne in heaven, probably laughing at both of us.

And then I met Bradley Knight.

My dad's church choir was recording a live worship album for a publishing company in Nashville. The label execs hired this young 23-year-old genius from South Carolina to play keys, arrange, and orchestrate the project. He stole my heart from my perch on the front row of the choir. We spent the weekend in each other's company during the live recording, bonding over quotes from the grossly underappreciated movie *Three Amigos*.

(This is the mark of true love.) A month later he came to visit me. He walked off the plane and told me he wanted to marry me. And that was that. At the ripe ages of 24 and 19 (respectively), Bradley and I were married in June of 2002. My visions of world tours and music videos and Times Square with Carson Daly took a backseat to my leading role as a wife. My dreams were still in the car with me, but Bradley Knight was at the wheel.

The day after our honeymoon, we moved to Dallas where my husband had been hired by a megachurch to write and arrange their music. With my family back in Colorado, and Bradley's family planted in South Carolina, our first few years of marriage were spent getting to know each other and strengthening our foundation as a new couple. These were sweet and difficult days for us. Sweet because we were alone. Difficult because we were lonely. It was hard for me to make friends with other married couples as a 19-year-old. I had much more in common with the girls in the youth group than the ladies in the Young Married's Bible Study at our church. I would much rather meet up at the mall with the 17 and 18-year-olds than attend a dinner party with the twenty-somethings. I soon found out, however, that becoming a mother was the great equalizer. It doesn't matter how old you are, when you pop out a baby you become part of an exclusive club called the "No Sleep Sorority."

After three years of marriage, against all my expectations, God blessed us with our first daughter, Ava Kathleen. She was a Mary Poppins baby: practically perfect in every way. She slept through the night at six weeks old. She never fussed. She was a great eater. Ava was a pure delight. Eighteen months later, we welcomed our second daughter, Greta Joy. She was yet another gift of Mary Poppins perfection. She also slept through the night at six weeks old. She was compliant and easy and content. Greta was our joy. And our family of four was complete. (That chuckling you hear? It's God.) A family of four was doable. A family of four traveled easily. A family of four was convenient. A family of four was affordable. Nobody stares at a family of four. Nobody feels sorry for a family of four. We lived in the happy land of "Family of Four" for two years.

Then I got pregnant on birth control.

IF THIS PART OF MY STORY IS PAINFUL FOR YOU

I'm going to take a breath and pause my story right here. I want to speak to those of you who may be experiencing infertility. You may find it excruciating to read my story because of your unfulfilled longing for a baby. You're currently contemplating slamming this book shut and cramming it into the bottom of your sock drawer, never to see the light of day again. And rightfully so. How is it that some women who never dream of motherhood (like myself) can get pregnant on birth control and procreate like it's a piece of cake? They literally cannot keep themselves from conceiving. It seems like they can sneeze and a baby miraculously appears. Meanwhile other women turn their bodies into a walking science experiment—poking and prodding, testing and tweaking hormones month after month only to be pulled under the water of despair, gasping for air in a tidal wave of disappointment over and over again. Or maybe they're able to (finally!) conceive, but a single sonogram fails to produce a heartbeat, and their glimmer of hope is extinguished. Why does this happen??? How is any of this fair??? I wish I knew. Don't you? I wish I had answers. But any kind of answer I could attempt to give you here would be fake and forced. And I've never been one for trite altruisms.

So instead of filling this page with hollow words highlighting what I don't know, I'll give you some rock solid truth spotlighting what I do know. I know we live in a broken world and life just flat out sucks sometimes. I know it often feels as if your prayers aren't making it past the ceiling. Life isn't fair. Life isn't easy. Life doesn't always go the way we expect it to. Life is messy. And it's messy for everybody in a myriad of ways. It's easy to feel overwhelmed and alone and overlooked and isolated when things turn out completely opposite of how you expected. It's easy to feel targeted or victimized or singled out in your grief. Like you're the only one who's ever felt this way. Like there's nobody else who could possibly understand what you're going through.

All of this is one big fat lie.

Here's the truth: we have a Savior who sympathizes with our hurts and weaknesses.[i] We have a Savior who became fully human to meet us where we are. We have a Savior who experienced every emotion—good and bad—we could possibly experience. We have a Savior who knows the exuberant joy and unfathomable pain that come from being human, trapped in skin, strolling this dusty earth wrought with disappointment. We have a Savior who knows. And He cares. Oh, how He cares. Read it

---

i Hebrews 4:15

for yourself:

> The Lord is gracious and compassionate,
> slow to anger and great in faithful love.
> The Lord is good to everyone;
> his compassion rests on all he has made.
> (Psalm 145:8-9)

> The Lord is near to the brokenhearted;
> he saves those crushed in spirit. (Psalm 34:18)

> Do not fear, for I am with you;
> do not be afraid, for I am your God.
> I will strengthen you; I will help you;
> I will hold on to you with my righteous right
> hand. (Isaiah 41:10)

> Come to me, all of you who are weary and
> burdened, and I will give you rest.
> (Matthew 11:28)

> I have told you these things so that in me you
> may have peace. You will have suffering in this
> world. Be courageous! I have conquered the
> world. (John 16:33)

No, I don't have all the answers to give you; because, same as you, there are some things I'll never understand this side of heaven. All I know is my God has an endless supply of comfort, grace, peace, strength, compassion, kindness, and love towards me and you. My Friend, if your nursery is empty today and your arms are longing to cradle a beloved baby, I pray you will find rest in the tender embrace of Jesus. And I pray God will give you the very honorable desire of your heart.

While I cannot personally relate with the specific ache of your struggle to conceive, I can absolutely empathize with you. My sister experienced infertility for seven years. While I was pushing out babies faster than you can say "prenatal vitamins," Janie was at home giving herself hormone shots and tracking every day of her cycle with stealth precision, only to be hit with disappointment month in and month out—for seven whole years. If I can offer you any hope, it's this: my sister is now the mother of four beautiful children, all of whom she birthed. God heard her cry and honored her faithfulness. And through the gift of modern medicine, He gave her the very honorable desire of her heart. I believe, dear Friend, if God has given you a yearning or a dream to become a mother, He will fulfill it according to His good plan. Hold onto His promises. Keep praying. Keep believing. Keep boldly approaching His throne with confidence. Keep crying out to Him. Keep the faith. And you can take this to the bank: God never initiates anything He doesn't intend to complete. He is the alpha AND the omega. He is the beginning AND the end. He is the author AND the finisher. "He who calls you is faithful; he will do it."[ii] (Yes, this is the second time I've quoted this verse and it probably won't be the last. You might as well go ahead and memorize it.)

Are you still with me sweet, beautiful, hopeful soon-to-be mother? Can you continue this journey with me? You are beyond

---

ii   1 Thessalonians 5:24

valuable and your presence here is much needed.

THE DEATH OF THE COOL MOM

I told you in the very first sentence of this book that I don't like kids. I wasn't lying. I never had plans for a large family, because I never knew when a record label executive might randomly call me out of the blue, offer me a million-dollar contract and a Vegas residency. I had to stay ready. And that included not having a minivan full of kids. I wasn't equipped to handle three or more children. Cool Moms don't have more than two kids. You can't change my mind about this.

If you are reading this today and you have three or more children and you are still grasping at the straws of your coolness, you need to stop. The gig is up for us. Our grass has withered. Our flower has faded. Our next round of awesomeness will hit all of us when these brats finally leave the house and turn out to be wildly successful adults with thriving businesses and fat 401K's and vacation homes on Nantucket where their mothers can spend the entire summer undisturbed because they were parented by absolute legends. *That's* when we'll be awesome again. But now is not our time.

When I found out I was pregnant with a third baby while on birth control, I cried actual tears. And they weren't happy tears. Two little pink lines made my "Family of Four" fantasy life vanish into thin air. Meanwhile, my husband was thrilled and congratulating himself for "getting one past the goalie." In all my ridiculous distress, there remained the hope of a silver lining: surely God surprised us with this pregnancy to bless us with a boy. A boy to carry on the Knight family name. A boy to balance out our estrogen-filled home. A boy to cheer for in every sport at which he had no choice but to be naturally gifted. A boy whose musical genius would rival his father's. A boy who would steal his mother's heart. Surely God was giving us a man-child, a male heir to our kooky kingdom. *Surely, that was the reason.*

Our third daughter, Harper Ryan, was born in June of 2009. A month later, my husband become surgically unable to father another child. We chopped down the only tree in our forest. (Bradley loves that phrase.) Because I was DONE. We were tapping out. Three girls would be it for us. No more children. Selah. (Yes, that's a distant celestial giggle you're hearing.)

Harper was not a Mary Poppins. Harper was a thug. And it was my fault. I was so exhausted from having three babies in four years that my parenting skills went out the window. Whatever Harper wanted, Harper got. Is she screaming for the brand-new toy that Greta just got for her birthday? *Give it to her immediately, Greta.* Is she sobbing because she doesn't want the gourmet dinner I made for her? *Give her some candy and shut her up already.* Is she having a total melt down because I happened to look at her the wrong way? *Please allow me to kneel at your feet and beg forgiveness.* Whenever Harper cried (she was never not crying), we all scrambled to answer her beck and call. She was our master. She was the boss. She was in control. Harper single-handedly affirmed our decision not to have any more children. And, because I'm a saint, I allowed Harper to live.

I'm not sure exactly when the transformation occurred, but eventually Harper became positively lovely—like her older sisters. She developed a quick sense of humor, a sharp mind, a sensitive heart, and meticulous manners. To this day, Harper Ryan is an absolutely delightful human being in every way imaginable. Thank You, God.

PROPHESYING OVER OUR CHILDREN

One day, while Harper was still little, she crawled into my lap as I was sitting at the kitchen table reading the book of Isaiah. The Spirit of God very clearly impressed upon my heart the passage I was reading was meant as a prophetic blessing for her and her sisters. These specific verses are describing Jesus, but I love praying them over my kids; because, aren't our kids supposed to look like Jesus?

> The Spirit of the Lord God is on me,
> because the Lord has anointed me
> to bring good news to the poor.
> He has sent me to heal the brokenhearted,
> to proclaim liberty to the captives
> and freedom to the prisoners;
> to proclaim the year of the Lord's favor,
> and the day of our God's vengeance;
> to comfort all who mourn,
> to provide for those who mourn in Zion;
> to give them a crown of beauty instead of ashes,
> festive oil instead of mourning,
> and splendid clothes instead of despair.
> And they will be called righteous trees,
> planted by the Lord to glorify him.

(Isaiah 61:1-4)

Moms, let's prophecy this over our children. May the Spirit of the Lord always be on them and with them. May they be agents of good news to the poor and desolate. May they comfort the brokenhearted and proclaim the freedom we have in Christ. May they abide in the Lord's favor. May their lives be marked with a crown of beauty and the oil of gladness. May they be righteous trees planted by the Lord to glorify Him. Let's boldly declare this over our kids. *That* is what all the Cool Moms are doing.

I was very young when I became a mother. I was unqualified and ill-equipped. I had no clue what I was doing half the time. I was exhausted and frazzled and overwhelmed. But I prayed to my God. And I stayed in my Bible. I had the audacity to believe what I read. I white knuckled every promise I could find—both for me and my children.

Harper eventually settled down and we eventually settled into a predictable routine as a family of five. We weren't cool. But we were comfortable. We were settled. We were complete. (Hahahahahahaha!)

chapter 3

COULD YOU REPEAT THAT *Jesus?*

It's funny how God has a way of disrupting our comfort. I've discovered He does His greatest disrupting when He's on the brink of pushing us into our calling. Our comfort was completely demolished in March of 2012.

Bradley and I were facing a difficult mountain and found ourselves in a season of intense prayer. Mountains take on various shapes and sizes, in each of our lives. I'm intentionally leaving out the specifics of our dilemma because I want you, Friend, to see your own obstacle here in my story. Our problems will look different from one another's. But make no mistake, while we live on this earth, we will all encounter our fair share of dangers, toils, and snares.

At this same time, Bradley and I were reading Mark Batterson's *The Circle Maker*. This book should come with a warning label: Dangerous Content. Do not read it unless you are prepared for serious breakthrough in your life. It is a blueprint for praying through your trial and grabbing hold of heaven. We implemented the principles laid out in this book: we identified our specific Jericho, we circled our problem, we claimed God's promises, and we prayed through. Boy, did we pray through.

Here's what Batterson has to say on the subject:

> Our generation desperately needs to rediscover
> the difference between praying for and praying
> through. There are certainly circumstances where
> praying for something will get the job done…But
> there are also situations where you need to grab
> hold of the horns of the altar and refuse to let
> go until God answers….Praying through is all
> about consistency. It's circling Jericho so many
> times it makes you dizzy…Praying through is all
> about intensity. [It] doesn't just bend God's ear; it
> touches the heart of your heavenly Father.[1]

As far as our prayer life was concerned, our Jericho marching had left us deliriously dizzy.

One particular evening, I was alone in my bedroom, crying out to God for help with our mountain. I was begging Him to remove the problem, pouring out my heart to Him, and praying through the thing. As I was praying, I heard the most incredible sound. It wasn't audible, but it was crystal clear. One single world.

Adoption.

Adoption??? This word made absolutely zero sense to me. How in the world was adoption going to help us conquer the giant in front of us? What did adoption have to do with anything?! It seemed as if God had become distracted from the task at hand. I'd been lamenting, pleading with Him to fix our circumstance, and the answer He gave me was *adoption???*

Oh gosh, but God didn't stop there. He had a couple more

terrifying words to add:

Two children.

And this, dear Friend, is the point where I assumed God had completely lost His mind. He certainly wasn't asking me to adopt two kids. Remember when I told you in the first sentence of the first chapter of this book I don't like kids? And then I told you I'm not equipped to parent more than two children? So, I was already a walking miracle in that regard. I told you that it is an absolute impossibility to have three or more kids and be a Cool Mom. And now here I was staring down the barrel of the loaded gun called "Mom of Five." A mom of five is the disgruntled ringmaster of a dysfunctional circus. She is a comedy of errors. She is a freakshow. A mom of five has no life. She lives buried under a mountain of laundry. She never goes to the bathroom by herself. She forgets her own name. She gets to take a shower exactly 1.75 times per month. A mom of five is the worst. Surely God wasn't calling me to be a mom of five.

The trouble with an intense season of praying through is that your ear is acutely attuned to the voice of the Lord. When He speaks, you hear Him loud and clear. There was no denying God's call to me: Adopt two children.

Once I took a deep breath and calmed down and acknowledged I had undoubtedly heard from God, I realized there was another hurdle still to be quelled: I had to tell my husband.

I approached Bradley with much fear and trembling. We had never discussed adoption in earnest. I had no idea what his reaction would be. All I knew is that we had made it surgically impossible for us to have any more children. Because we were

D-O-N-E. And on this night, with my heart pounding in my chest, I had to inform him that we, in fact, were not done.

Bradley could have said no, and that would've shut down the entire operation. But because you're holding a book in your hand, pages filled with the rest of our story, you've probably guessed Bradley didn't say no. In fact, when I told him God had given me the word "adoption," his response was "I know." And when I told him God had made it clear we would be adopting two children, his response was "I know."

Bradley already knew. Because God had already told him, too.

So with tears spilling down our cheeks, we grabbed each other's hand and walked upstairs to our guest bedroom. We knelt down on the floor and immediately dedicated the room to the two children God would be bringing to our family. We didn't know who they were. We didn't know where they were. We didn't know when we'd meet them. We didn't know how it would all work out. We only knew that we had heard from God, and with a million questions swirling around in our minds, we said "Yes."

MOUNTAIN AFTER MOUNTAIN

Friend, do you remember the mountain we were facing at the beginning of this chapter? The obstacle we had been praying through? The day after saying *yes* to adoption, God totally and completely handled our problem. He eliminated it. Wiped it out. Miraculously. We had been pleading with God to remove a burden, and in His lovingkindness, He removed it only to give us an even weightier assignment.

Has this ever happened to you? Have you ever conquered one mountain only to find Everest staring at you on the other side? Has God ever calmed your storm only to invite you to step out of your perfectly comfortable boat and walk on the water with Him? What a thrill it is to walk with Jesus through it all.

Moses was no stranger to mountains. He would conquer one obstacle only to be smacked in the face with another. He led the Israelites through plagues and the Passover. He liberated God's people out of slavery in Egypt only to be pinned in between a sea and Pharoah's army. He marched the multitudes across the Red Sea on bone-dry ground only to be floundering in a wilderness with no water or food. He cried out to God and bread miraculously fell from the sky and water poured out of a rock. It seems as if Moses could barely catch his breath between battles.

I wonder if the psalmist had Moses in mind when he penned Psalm 84:5-7:

> Happy are the people whose strength is in you,
> whose hearts are set on pilgrimage.
> As they pass through the Valley of Tears,
> they make it a source of spring water;
> even the autumn rain will cover it with blessings.
> They go from strength to strength;
> each appears before God in Zion.

They go from strength to strength.

We were in a "strength to strength" moment. God had graciously and supernaturally answered our desperate prayers, and immediately led us into our next mission. He gave us all the strength we needed and then He lovingly gave us more strength.

Paul puts it this way: "For God is working in you, giving you the desire and the power to do what pleases him."[i] In other words, God calls us and simultaneously strengthens us to fulfill His calling. Because He knows how frail we are, our weaknesses don't surprise Him. And during this period of our lives, Bradley and I needed all the strength we could get.

UGANDA BE KIDDING ME

At this exact same time, my mother happened to be on a mission trip to the country of Uganda. She was serving alongside a man named Kasadha Emmanuel (Emma). Emma was the founder of Care Medical Center in Kampala, where women with unexpected pregnancies receive free treatment, prayer, and counseling. Many women end up choosing life for their babies through this ministry. Due to my mother's work in the country, Uganda immediately popped up in the back of my mind upon hearing God's call of adoption. What if it wasn't a coincidence my mother was in that specific country at this specific time? What if God was calling us to Uganda? What if our babies were there?

But I quickly silenced myself and suppressed the idea. I didn't want to assume anything. The truth is, sometimes I'm really great at hearing the voice of the Lord, and sometimes I make up crap in my head. And even though I was in an intense season of prayer, I didn't feel ready to trust every little nudge or whisper I heard. I needed God to keep shouting at me—clearly and audibly, if necessary. Bradley and I had made ourselves

---

i   Philippians 2:13 NLT

completely available to God. Our children could be anywhere. When we said yes to adoption, we were saying yes to complete surrender and total obedience. We were ready to go anywhere. I wanted to stay open to all possibilities. And so, we kept praying.

The next week, I was picking up my oldest daughter from a choir rehearsal at our church when I saw a white woman carrying a gorgeous black baby girl on the far side of the sanctuary. At this point, Bradley and I had been worship leaders at our church for 10 years. Although it was a massive place, I felt like I knew most everybody. But I didn't know this woman. I can't accurately explain how utterly compelled I was to run after her. My feet couldn't get me to her fast enough. I felt the urge to jump from the back of a pew and make an attempt at flying. When I finally reached her, I lost all decorum and any social graces I may have possessed and without taking a breath said, "Hi my name is Holly Knight we haven't met before but my husband and I lead worship here what is your name it's so nice to meet you where is your baby from?"

The woman's name was Dara and her baby's name was Abigail. Abigail was just adopted from Uganda, along with her sister Vicky, through the aid of Kasadha Emma at Care Medical Center in Kampala, where my mother was currently working. And yes, Dara would be happy to give me her phone number so I could call her later and aggressively ask 20,000 questions.

Y'all. I can be dense. Stupid. And stubborn to a fault. After my divine meeting with Dara, I proceeded to get in my car with Ava and drive home from church, questioning God the entire way: *Are you actually calling us to adopt from Uganda? This is too big of a task for us! God, you can't be serious?! Do you even know what you're doing?! Are you sure we're not meant to adopt domestically? Are you really sending us to Africa? God, this is huge! Did I hear you clearly? Could you please repeat yourself? I need another sign. Please, can you give me another sign?*

God gave me another sign.

When I arrived home, five minutes later, my little diaper-clad thug of a toddler ran to meet me as I entered the house, wearing a t-shirt I had never seen. It said: Uganda. God literally wrote the name of the country on Harper's chest.

My persistent prayers for repeated confirmation were answered. God clearly spoke to me because I begged Him to clearly speak to me. There was no more doubting. No more questioning. No more wondering. From that day on, our mission was clear: we would absolutely be adopting two babies from the country of Uganda.

chapter 4

REVELATION AND
Red Tape

We needed to break the news to our kids. How on earth were we to inform our young daughters God had chosen our family to adopt two babies from Uganda? How do we go about explaining we've made a decision that will affect them for the rest of their lives? Or that we were taking a leap of faith and they had no choice in the matter? By now, we were in the habit of praying through everything. So we prayed through.

One evening while I was cooking dinner, I heard the Holy Spirit whisper: *Now.* I dropped everything, found Bradley, and told him that it was time to tell the kids. Bradley and I were used to approaching each other with directives from the Lord. So, he was not shocked by my announcement and readily agreed. We said a quick prayer together, then found our little chicks and gathered them around the kitchen table. Ava was 7, Greta was 5, and Harper was 2.

> Me: Girls, did you know the Bible tells us that we are supposed to help take care of widows and orphans?
> Girls: Yes!
> Me: Who can tell me what it means to be an

orphan?

Greta: It means that you don't have any parents.

Me: That's right. How do you think we can help take care of orphans?

Ava: We could adopt an orphan!

Me: That's a great idea!

Ava: Hey! Let's adopt two orphans! From Africa!

Me: *Jaw on the floor.*

It was that easy. God, in His gentleness and kindness, made it Ava's divine idea to adopt two babies from Africa. He immediately invited my small children to be an integral part of His grand plan. He cared enough about the feelings of three little girls and how His calling on their parents would have a profound impact on their precious lives. He was ever so loving and tender with them. My children matter to my Savior. I'm crying as I write this, even now. God's faithfulness to my kids is something I'll never get over.

A BRACELET OF THREE STRANDS

Around this same time, I was reading my Bible one morning when I looked down at my left wrist and felt God speak to me. I was wearing a bracelet my mother had brought home from Uganda a few weeks earlier. It was made of three strings of beads fashioned out of garbage—a traditional way to construct beautiful jewelry in many African countries. As I looked down at the three strands of my bracelet, I heard the Holy Spirit tell me there would be three children adopted from Uganda.

SAY WHAT?????

In my mind I could hear a car come to a screeching halt and see smoking tires leaving black skid marks on the pavement. You can imagine my surprise at this revelation. Remember, God had CLEARLY told us to adopt two children. He even let it be Ava's idea! Surely He wasn't changing His mind. Does God change His mind?

I held onto this word from the Lord and kept it to myself. Because, as I've mentioned, I'm also prone to make up crap in my head. I had no clue what any of this even meant.

Until I had lunch with my dear friend, Dianna.

Dianna and I met as newlyweds, working in administrative positions at our church. Her spunk and personality matched mine perfectly, and we had an instant connection. We each gave birth to our three children around the same time. We lived in the same neighborhood. Our kids were best friends. We were a crew.

I'll never forget our meal together, sitting across from one another at California Pizza Kitchen. With tears in her eyes, Dianna told me she and Josh had also been called to adopt a child from Uganda. Specifically, a boy. Because of the word God had given me, I was able to affirm and edify Dianna's calling. I could encourage her in the monumental decision to step out on faith, just as we had done. God was doing a work in her family's life, just as He was in mine.

Dianna's son was the third strand of my bracelet. Her story is forever intertwined with mine, which you will discover as you continue reading about our journey.

DEATH BY PAPERWORK

I've learned when God calls you to complete an amazingly large assignment, He's also asking you to accomplish a million small tasks along the way. Trusting Him with the big picture ultimately consists of obeying Him with every slight step you take as you follow Him on this journey. Our faithful, consistent brush strokes will one day yield an elaborate tapestry of God's design.

That's how I'm choosing to remember and attempt to describe the never-ending, all-consuming, suffocating mountain of paperwork required for adoption. If you've been through this process, you know exactly what I'm talking about. Just when you think you've made a dent chipping away at some of the applications and forms, a new pile appears out of nowhere. And the cycle keeps repeating itself until you die.

I remember having next-level anxiety regarding our medical exams, and I am typically not an anxious person. The practices and procedures involved with adopting children are necessary and good. Crucial checks and balances are put into place for the safety and protection of everyone involved. I'm grateful for this. However, at the time, it scared me to death. Along with the suffocating paperwork, our family had multiple rounds of doctors' appointments, physicals, and bloodwork. Every time I, or one of my kids, had to get a medical test of some sort, I would experience a wave of panic as I awaited results. What if one of us has an illness that disqualifies us from adopting? What if this slight pain in my abdomen is a tumor and I'm going to die tomorrow? What if Bradley has a rare, incurable cancer and our plans are thwarted? See what I mean about making up crap in my head? The "what-ifs" I had conjured up were given way too much real estate in my brain.

Do you ever find yourself inventing ways to sabotage your calling by allowing fear to reign in your mind? I find I'm most prone to do this after receiving clear direction from the Lord. I'm a professional when it comes to disqualifying myself from what God has asked me to accomplish, because I know what's on the inside of me. I know how flawed I am. I know how insignificant, limited, and ordinary I am. I naturally assume someone else could complete my mission better than I could, and with much more style and grace.

MOSES FELT THE SAME WAY

Remember Moses, our friend who led the Israelites through the plagues and the wilderness and the Red Sea? In the third and fourth chapters of Exodus, we read about God calling Moses to a large task—an assignment more monumental than any human could possibly complete. And Moses tried his darndest to disqualify himself. He had a few "what-ifs" of his own:

> But Moses asked God, "Who am I that I should go to Pharaoh and that I should bring the Israelites out of Egypt?" (Exodus 3:11)
> Then Moses asked God, "If I go to the Israelites and say to them, 'The God of your ancestors has sent me to you,' and they ask me, 'What is his name?' what should I tell them?" (Exodus 3:13)

Moses answered, "What if they won't believe me and will not obey me but say, 'The Lord did not appear to you'?" (Exodus 4:1)

But Moses replied to the Lord, "Please, Lord, I have never been eloquent—either in the past or recently or since you have been speaking to your servant—because my mouth and my tongue are sluggish." (Exodus 4:10)

Moses said, "Please, Lord, send someone else." (Exodus 4:13)

Moses had some legitimate concerns about his lack of qualifications. He was a nobody. He had no power. He had a speech impediment. I love how honest he was in Exodos 4:13, flat out asking God to send someone else. How sublimely relatable. God was patient with Moses. He was long-suffering, but firm. Just as He is with you and me. In all my needless stress and absurd freak outs, God never wavered. He gently kept reassuring me of my calling and of His faithfulness. He kept nudging me to obedience.

Which, unfortunately, included that infinite stack of paperwork and red tape.

DESIGNER FIRE EXTINGUISHERS

Nothing will leave you feeling exposed like a home study visit. I mean, *nothing.*

I was given a detailed list of elaborate instructions on how to prepare for this visit and I checked it twice. Then I checked it thrice. At this appointment, somebody was going to invade my world, walk through my home, go through my pantry, dig through my medicine cabinet, examine every closet, inspect the cleanliness of every room, interview me, Bradley, and our daughters, to decide if we were fit as a family to bring adopted children into our home. No pressure. Actually, *all the pressure.* Everything had to be perfect. I alphabetized my prescription drugs and placed them in a cabinet high out of reach of my kids. I organized and reorganized every drawer. I decluttered every nook. I decorated every shelf. I bought a *designer fire extinguisher* because I thought it was pretty and would be more impressive on my kitchen counter. I cleaned my baseboards for Pete's sake. I coached my children on every possible question they may receive from the home study agent, including this fun question: How do your parents punish you when you get in trouble? Right answer: They take away privileges. Wrong answer: They spank our butts. This question took a little extra coaching. I don't even care if you're judging me right now. It is what it is.

As you might imagine, I was a ball of nerves on the day of the visit. I had gone over every possible horrific scenario in my head. I was becoming an expert in this practice. The woman who arrived to investigate us was young and kind. She was soft-spoken and patient with my girls. She was thoughtful and contemplative with Bradley and me. She asked appropriate questions and took thorough notes. The entire visit lasted about two hours. I was both relieved and offended she never once looked inside my squeaky-clean pantry or witnessed my pharmaceuticals in all their alphabetized splendor. She didn't even comment on my fabulous fire extinguisher. My sparkling baseboards escaped her notice. How rude.

I had once again let myself get wrapped up and carried away in superfluous details. I was concerned about a perfectly clean kitchen; the agent was interested in the solidity of my marriage. I was obsessed over immaculate pantries, closets, and cabinets; she was focused on the mental and emotional health of my children. It seemed as if the agent was less concerned with the periphery of our house and more interested in the heart of our home.

You may or may not be adopting children any time soon. You may never have to open your family up to inspection and scrutiny like we did. But now is a good time to take inventory for yourself. Even as I recount my story and laugh over the absurd things that caused me to fret about our home study, I'm convicted over my jumbled priorities:

- Am I needlessly obsessing over details that don't matter?
- Am I more concerned with how my family's photos turn out on social media than I am with strengthening my marriage and shepherding the hearts of my children?
- Am I a slave to the schedule I create because I value busyness over rest?

These questions are not rhetorical. Thank God. I fear my honest answers would be incriminating. I'm guilty of all the above. But when all is said and done, I want to cultivate deep, healthy roots in our home and not be satisfied by simply displaying beautiful blossoms that will quickly fade. It's good to check in with ourselves once in a while and see if there are any areas that need to be brought back into alignment with what really matters: a flourishing family that pleases God.

MATCHED

The abundance of paperwork, every form we completed, every doctor's appointment we attended, every hoop we jumped through, it all came down to one moment: being matched with our Ugandan children. The email appeared in my inbox while I was at the pediatrician with Harper. My stomach flipped and my heart stopped beating. I didn't have the guts to open it there in that office by myself. I was about to see pictures of my children for the first time.

I raced home and met Bradley at the house. Once again, we gathered our little chicks around us, sat down at the computer, and clicked on the email. And there, staring at us through the screen, were two of the most beautiful children I had ever seen. Mumwata James was around two years old, and Akansasira Joan appeared slightly younger. My daughters *oohed* and *aahed,* declaring they had never seen cuter babies. They were captivated by the dark chocolate hue of their skin and eyes. We all cried together and agreed we couldn't wait to hug and kiss these two perfect angels.

At that moment, all the anxiety of the past few months melted away. I had a picture in my inbox to hold onto. I had names for the unknown children with whom I was forming an intense bond in my heart. I had evidence that what we were tirelessly working towards was real—real-life babies, with real-life names and real-life faces.

My longing to hold these two children deepened by the hour. They were the first thing I thought of every morning. Their faces were the last images I focused on before falling asleep. I was perpetually distressed over what (or if) the babies were eating, how they were sleeping, how they were being treated. Not being in charge of their daily caretaking was both disheartening and maddening. I felt torn between two places: Dallas and Uganda. This feeling moved right in and made itself at home.

And it stayed for a while.

The last piece of the puzzle required for us to travel to Uganda was an approval letter from U.S. Customs and Immigration stating we had permission to bring two immigrants back to the United States. This letter was delivered to us on Wednesday, August 22, 2012.

It was time to go to Africa.

chapter 5

ONE-WAY *Tickets*

We purchased one-way plane tickets departing for Uganda on Monday, August 27. We had 5 days to get ready for the trip of a lifetime.

How does one prepare for a journey to the other side of the world in five days? I don't have an absolute answer for this. I still don't know how we accomplished it all. All I know is I pushed every feeling and emotion to the side, put my head down, and worked my fingers to the bone.

My top priority was the well-being of my daughters. At the time, Bradley and I didn't have any family living near us. We had an incredible community, and our village came through for us. Our plan quickly fell into place: my friend and mentor Lisa would stay with the girls for the first week, my mother would travel down from Kansas for week two, and my sister would fly in from Colorado for our third week away. We were not anticipating being in Uganda for more than three weeks. (Spoiler alert: I was in Uganda for longer than three weeks. Much longer.)

I assembled all pertinent information regarding my girls in a three-ring binder, two inches thick: daily schedules, ballet class, soccer practice, game schedules, field maps, nap times, bath time routines, kids' choir schedule, Mother's Day Out instructions, school hours, carpool drop-off and pick-up routes, potty training instructions for Harper, meal suggestions and recipes, pediatrician contact info, medical insurance details, necessary power of attorney letters, play date schedules, local moms to call for back-up, and the location of my infamously alphabetized prescription drugs should they be required.

And yet, I wish someone would've given me a list of instructions on how to prepare myself mentally and emotionally to be separated from my babies for an indefinite amount of time. There was no three-ring binder for my aching heart. No plan in place for how I was supposed to continue breathing without my children. No scheduled return flight home.

Amidst the frantic planning and preparations, my brain was having a difficult time reconciling the intense excitement and extreme sorrow I was simultaneously experiencing. My best coping mechanism was to temporarily ignore my feelings and dismiss my emotions. I was in survival mode.

We bought oversized suitcases and trunks to pack for our trip. Friends gifted us with clothing, toys, and diapers for the two babies waiting for us in Uganda. We packed an entire bag full of medical supply donations to be given to Kasadha Emma at Care Medical Center. Ava, Greta, and Harper added a special toy or trinket to share with their new brother and sister. We were advised to pack our own food and snacks to eat while in our hotel room. I loaded up on dry ramen noodles, instant oatmeal packets, crackers, cookies, dried fruit, and nuts. I packed 2 loaves of fresh bread into a shoe box, along with a jar of Smucker's strawberry jam and Jif Creamy Peanut Butter. PB&J would become my manna.

NEVER ONCE

That Sunday, Bradley and I led worship at our church one last time before our departure. I don't know why I even bothered to put makeup on my face that morning because I cried it all off within the first five minutes of the first service. Leading our congregation in joyful worship was something I loved to do every weekend. But this Sunday was different. This Sunday, I was leading from utter sorrow, unspeakable excitement, overwhelming fear, and total submission. I was worshiping from a place of complete desperation on the Lord.

God, in His providence, had us sing a specific, prophetic song—"Never Once," by Matt Redman:

> Standing on this mountaintop
> Looking just how far we've come
> Knowing that for every step
> You were with us
>
> Kneeling on this battle ground
> Seeing just how much You've done
> Knowing every victory
> Was Your power in us
>
> Scars and struggles on the way
> But with joy our hearts can say
> Yes, our hearts can say

Never once did we ever walk alone
Never once did You leave us on our own
You are faithful, God, You are faithful

Every step we are breathing in Your grace
Evermore we'll be breathing out Your praise
You are faithful, God, You are faithful[2]

God knew. He knew the rocky road on which we were about to travel. He knew the depth of the valley He was about to bring us through. He knew we were about to enter a battle we were much too weak to fight. He knew how overwhelmed I felt. He knew how scared to death I was. He knew how ecstatic I was to meet my Ugandan children. He knew how I dreaded leaving my biological daughters behind. He knew I was leaving everything familiar with a one-way ticket to Africa, not knowing when I would return. He knew it all. And in His sovereignty, He had me lead our church in a song that declared His never-ending faithfulness. As I worshiped God, I was reminding myself of His trustworthiness, His constancy, His steadfastness. God was encouraging me as I edified Him. He gave me this song to hold onto through the coming weeks. A token to remind me He had called me, He would be with me, and He would give me the victory. What a good God He is.

FIRST DAY OF SCHOOL

That next day, Monday, August 27, was Greta's first day of kindergarten, Ava's first day of 2nd grade, and Harper's first day of ballet class. It was also the day Bradley and I boarded our flight to Uganda. I had learned my lesson from the previous day and decided against putting makeup on my face. The tears started flowing on the way to school drop-off and didn't dry up for a solid 13 hours.

The first day of school (especially kindergarten!) is emotional, no matter how you slice it. But when you add on the fact I was going straight to the airport to fly to a foreign country, unsure of my return? Believe me when I say I caused a scene. I walked my precious Ava and Greta, pristinely clad in their plaid uniforms, through the front doors of their school and led them to each of their classrooms. I tried to keep myself composed for their sake, but my efforts were futile. I sobbed and snotted and snorted all over these little girls. And they let me. They didn't push me away. They knew we were leaving. Bradley was also crying, but he wasn't quite as hysterical as me.

I held onto my girls a little longer than I needed to. I kissed them a few more times than was necessary. I told them I loved them more than they would ever know. And then I let them go. I walked out of the building, weeping and praying, asking God how I was ever going to make it through this pain.

The agony of walking away from my children that day makes me recall another mother who must've known exactly how I felt: Hannah. How did she do it? How did Hannah let her child go? How did she miraculously give birth to Samuel after years of infertility and lovingly nurse him at her breast, only to take him to the temple and leave him there with Eli, the priest? How did she walk away from her long-awaited son, after dedicating him to the Lord? And how did she find the strength to pray this Spirit-filled prayer:

> For the foundations of the earth are the Lord's;
> he has set the world on them.
> He guards the steps of his faithful ones,
> but the wicked perish in darkness,
> for a person does not prevail by his own strength.
> Those who oppose the Lord will be shattered;
> he will thunder in the heavens against them.
> The Lord will judge the ends of the earth.
> He will give power to his king;
> he will lift up the horn of his anointed.
> (1 Samuel 2:8b–10)

The source of Hannah's strength can be found in her name. Hannah means "grace." Hannah had the courage and tenacity to leave her beloved son with Eli because she had the grace that accompanies obedience. She knew firsthand "He guards the steps of his faithful ones" (v 9, above). When we are faithful to follow wherever God leads us, He is faithful to provide the grace and strength required at every turn.

God's grace was with me and Bradley at school drop-off on that miserable Monday morning. His grace didn't remove our pain, but it gave us the strength to take another step. To put one foot in front of the other. To take another breath. To get in the car and drive to the airport. To trust His plan for us, even when it hurt. His unfailing grace accompanied our unwavering obedience.

AIRPORT EBENEZERS

I sat in the back seat next to Harper on the way to the airport, clutching her dimpled hand and quietly crying the entire way. Bradley was driving. My friend Lisa was sitting in the front passenger seat. I don't recall any words being spoken. None were necessary.

When we arrived at the airport, I clung to my baby for as long as I possibly could. Harper had just turned three years old. She couldn't fully comprehend where we were going, why we were leaving, or what we were doing. She was just thrilled to be spending some alone time with "Miss Lisa" and go to ballet class for the first time. I managed to keep myself together for her sake. She was too young to understand her mother's hysterics.

Watching Lisa pull away with my youngest daughter in the car was the final straw that broke the camel's back of this brokenhearted mommy. The levee busted open and the waterworks began in earnest. Y'all, I was a sloppy hot mess.

Once again, I began questioning God's call on our lives. *Did He actually ask us to buy one-way tickets to a foreign country and leave our young, impressionable daughters behind indefinitely? Would a loving God honestly ask us to do this? Is obeying God supposed to be this painful? Are we supposed to be this miserable? Were we doing the right thing? Did God see us? Could God really be trusted?* These were the questions going through my mind as we checked in for our three-legged flight from Dallas to Houston to London to Entebbe, Uganda.

As we got in line for TSA Security, I heard Bradley say, "Hey, Mark!" I looked up and saw Christian singer/songwriter Mark Harris and his wife, Jodie. I had a small fangirl moment because Mark was one-fourth of the group 4Him, whose records stayed on constant rotation in my house growing up. Thankfully, this provided a good distraction for me. Bradley and Mark had worked together remotely on a few projects in the past but had never met face-to-face. After we exchanged pleasantries, Mark and Jodie inquired as to where we were going and what we were doing. They could tell we were distraught (my swollen eyes, stuffy nose, and tear-stained face probably gave it away) and asked how they could pray for us. We quickly told them our story and how we were embarking on a crazy journey and had just kissed our kids goodbye. And there, in the airport security line, Mark and Jodie prayed over us, asking God to be with us every step of the way, that His power would be within us to overcome every obstacle, and that He would finish what He started in us.

My spirits instantly lifted. God was with us at the Dallas airport. For the first time all day, I felt like I could exhale. We said goodbye to our new friends, made it through security, and boarded our flight to Houston.

An hour later, we landed at Houston's Hobby airport. But our next flight to London departed from Houston's Bush Intercontinental airport. A minor dilemma.

I enlisted the help of my childhood friend, Jamie. She had moved to Houston from Denver to be near her father and was the perfect companion to drive us between airports. During the car ride, we engaged in encouraging conversation. Jamie reminded us of the faithfulness of God. She edified us and prayed for us.

Once again, God was with us at the Houston airport.

Our flight to London was long and uneventful. We landed in England in a complete mental fog, exhausted from emotional events of the previous day. As soon as we touched down, my phone pinged with a text from my longtime friend, Petrus, who had recently moved to the United Kingdom. He wanted to come meet us for our long layover. We linked up at a tiny pub next to the airport, where he brought us an invaluable gift: a box of Ben's Cookies. If you've never experienced the splendor of Ben's Cookies, there's no need to fret. These cookies will most definitely be served at the Marriage Supper of the Lamb, so you'll get to taste them eventually. They carry the shekinah glory of the Lord. One bite will change your life.

As it turned out, God was with us at the London airport, too. With our hearts and bellies full, we boarded our last flight to Uganda.

Friend, it is not lost on me that God showed up for us at every stop of our journey. Even as I questioned Him, doubting His faithfulness and skeptical of His calling, His plan was already in motion. By His design, Mark and Jodie were at airport security at the exact right time to pray for us. Jamie was willing and available to not only drive us through Houston, but to edify us and encourage us as we went. Petrus was in London, eager to meet us and bless us in a tangible way with Holy Ghost cookies. God had set up mile-markers of His love at every point, confirming His calling on us, establishing His presence with us, and fulfilling His purpose in us. God was with us.

In all my disbelief and uncertainty, God never failed to lovingly whisper to me:

Never once did you ever walk alone.
Never once did I leave you on your own.
I am faithful, Holly. I am faithful.

chapter 6

NEW COUNTRY,
Who Dis?

It was the smell that hit me first.

Deplaning down the stairs and onto the tarmac at Entebbe airport, after 26 hours of travel, all my senses were on high alert. The bright mid-day sun caused me to squint after being held hostage in a dark cabin for hours on end. There was a haze blanketing the luster of the day and a thick humidity nearly tangible. The handrails of the steps were damp from the moisture in the air. Across the runway, I could see luscious green fields, bursting with native vegetation. All around me, there were people with dazzling dark chocolate skin directing air crafts, pulling luggage from cargo units, busily working their jobs. Everything was new, different, foreign, and exciting. But it was the smell that caught me off guard.

The scent of the atmosphere was unlike anything I've ever experienced: a mixture of smoke, garbage, rain, grass, and a hint of sweetness. Sugar cane, maybe? The fragrance of the air was the chief indicator I was stepping into unfamiliar territory. I was entering a country where I was a foreigner, an alien, an outsider. I could no longer rely on the recognizable rhythms and convenient customs of life back in Texas. Other than my dear husband, I did not have the presence of family and friends to comfort me. I was no longer home.

It is my experience that radical, stubborn obedience to Christ often leads us into unknown lands, both literally and spiritually. In fact, I can't think of any example where someone surrenders their life to Jesus and gets to stay in their comfort zone. Fulfilling your purpose while remaining comfortable and complacent doesn't seem to add up in God's math.

I posed these questions to you in the first chapter, and I want to ask them again, just in case you've forgotten this is your story, too:

- What has God called you to do?
- What has He put in you to accomplish that is a million times bigger than you could imagine?
- What assignment is in front of you that scares the living daylights out of you and makes you break out in a cold sweat?
- What dream has God given you that seems impossible?

The truth of the matter is this: when you grab hold of the thing God has planned for you—when you've drawn a line in the sand and fully committed your life to His purpose—you've just accepted a one-way ticket to territory the likes of which you have never seen.

It is terrifying and it is glorious.

Your assignment may not include adopting children or stepping off a plane in a foreign country. It may not even include leaving your neighborhood. But following God at all costs will be thrilling and it will be uncomfortable.

LEADING LADIES

There are some incredible women of the Bible who exemplify this kind of tenacious surrender. Ruth comes to mind. Ruth obeyed a God she barely knew. Raised a Moabite, the God of Abraham, Isaac, and Jacob would've been a foreign deity to her. She was introduced to the true God of Israel when she married her first husband, Naomi's son. Ruth and Naomi both become widows within the first five verses of Ruth. After facing the pain and agony of losing her husband, going home to her family would've been the easy and obvious choice for Ruth. Seeking solace in the arms of her parents and siblings would have made sense. It would have been the convenient path. Instead of retreating and taking the easy road, Ruth becomes stubborn. She made the decision to stay with Naomi, and resolutely spoke these famous words recorded in Ruth 1:16-17:

> Don't plead with me to abandon you or to return and not follow you. For wherever you go, I will go, and wherever you live, I will live; your people will be my people, and your God will be my God. Where you die, I will die, and there I will be buried. May the Lord punish me, and do so severely, if anything but death separates you and me.

And with that declaration, the women made their way from Moab back to Israel.

Talk about surrender? Talk about finding yourself in a place you've never been before? Talk about guts? This is it. Ruth found herself in a new country, with new scenery, new scents, new foods, new customs. And upon arriving she had to quickly find a job, or she and Naomi would starve. Ruth learned to put one foot in front of the other. She navigated the unknown by doing the next right thing. And then the next. Instead of freaking out, or whining, or bemoaning her terrible fortune, Ruth put her head down and got to work. Which lead her to Boaz, the man who would marry Ruth and redeem Naomi's family heritage in Israel. Ruth's refusal to give in and go home led her to become the great-grandmother to King David, and ultimately a part of the genealogy of Jesus. Ruth's stubbornness in a foreign land carried eternal significance.

Esther also comes to mind. Following God didn't take her to a new country, it simply took her to a new house. Her grand prize for winning the Miss Persia beauty pageant was marrying King Xerxes and becoming queen, literally overnight. She moved into a new house, with new surroundings and new people. Esther was plucked from Jewish obscurity and planted in the royal residence. And for what purpose? Her own comfort and convenience? Hardly.

Esther could have kicked back and relaxed in her new palace, being waited on hand and foot. Her queenly position must have called for extraneous pampering. Every desire would have been indulged and gratified. She must have wanted for nothing. I'm in my late 30s and still haven't lost my baby weight from giving birth 12 years ago, but I would definitely risk utter humiliation and mass confusion and don a sensible tankini to enter a beauty pageant where the grand prize was becoming a coddled queen with a harem to serve me night and day. Where do I sign up?

But not Esther. She was on assignment.

Esther's obedience in her new territory involved opening her mouth and using her voice to save her people from execution at the risk of her own life. Esther's obedience meant she put everything on the line for the sake of an entire nation. Esther's obedience was founded in an unwavering belief that "perhaps she had come to her royal position for such a time as this."[i] And Esther's stubborn obedience was rewarded with favor from the king, and the saving of countless Jewish lives. Esther's obedience mattered.

And I can't help but think of Mary, the mother of Jesus. Mary's surrender to God came in the form of an unplanned pregnancy. She found herself in the wilderness of loneliness, judgment, and fear of the unknown. *As a teenager.* Mary's story has become more tender to me now that my daughters are teens. Mary was around my daughter's age when her life was upended by an angel's announcement. Her foreign land looked a lot like swollen breasts and ankles, stretch marks, morning sickness, raging hormones, sleepless nights, and the judgmental stares of those who didn't understand the unspeakable majesty inhabiting her womb. Mary's obedience in a new territory embodied waking up every morning, tuning out the world's criticisms, and choosing to believe what God said about her:

- She was chosen, not forsaken.
- God was for her, not against her.
- God would never leave her.
- God would provide for her and protect her.
- She was blessed among women.

---

i   Esther 4:14

• She was, indeed, carrying the Savior of the world.

I still marvel at the faith it must've taken this young girl to pray this prayer of praise and surrender to God recorded in the first chapter of Luke:

> My soul praises the greatness of the Lord, and my spirit rejoices in God my Savior, because he has looked with favor on the humble condition of his servant. Surely, from now on all generations will call me blessed, because the Mighty One has done great things for me, and his name is holy. His mercy is from generation to generation on those who fear him. He has done a Mighty deed with his arm; he has scattered the proud because of the thoughts of their hearts; he has topped the mighty from their thrones and exalted the lowly. He has satisfied the hungry with good things and sent the rich away empty. He has helped his servant Israel, remembering his mercy to Abraham and his descendants forever, just as he spoke to our ancestors. (vv. 46-55)

I don't think I need to elaborate on the significance of Mary's obedience in a new land. Her unplanned pregnancy wasn't actually unplanned. It was ordained before the foundation of time. There will never be a greater gift to this universe than the baby boy whom young Mary gave birth to that glorious night in an animal barn in Bethlehem. Mary's steadfast obedience and tenacious teenage faith in the midst of the unknown literally changed the world.

EVERYDAY WOMEN

But I'm not Ruth. I'm not Esther. And I'm definitely not Mary. And neither are you. We're normal, everyday women, not queens or royalty. We live in houses or apartments and wake up each day to care for our children or head off to work. Maybe we're concerned with closing the next big deal. Maybe we're stressed over what to cook for dinner tonight. Because dinner occurs every night without fail and we're exhausted, and these kids are bottomless pits and maybe we'll just have pizza delivered for the ninth time this week. We're mere mortals just trying to get it done. How are we expected to navigate foreign lands? How do we find routine and rhythm in the unknown land of total surrender to God? How do we roll with the punches the enemy is sure to throw once he realizes we're on assignment for the Lord? Let's take our cue from the heroines of this chapter:

1. We can do the next right thing, like Ruth.

Following God rarely involves pomp and circumstance. For Ruth, it involved finding a field and gathering leftover barley dropped by the harvesters. It involved sweat. It involved hard work she thought no one saw. It involved an achy back and tired feet. It involved making the next right choice, even in the midst of obscurity.

What is the next right thing for you? It may be waking up tomorrow and choosing to forgive that person who wronged you yet again. It may be showing up at a thankless job, knowing you're called to be a light in the darkness. It may be staying true to the vows you made on your wedding day, even if your marriage is on the rocks. It may be walking away from an abusive relationship and believing you're worthy of love. It may be getting on your knees in prayer for the millionth time for that child who is away from the Lord. Sweet Friend, what is the next right thing for you? Do it. Obey God. Surrender to Him. And then do the next right thing after that.

2. *We can use our voices, like Esther.*

In the midst of Esther's unfamiliar circumstances, with the fate of her people at stake, she chose to speak up and ask the king for mercy—even at the risk of losing her life. And her request was granted. I wonder how many blessings and miracles I've missed out on in my life simply because I haven't opened my mouth and asked for them? When we're in a new place, *especially when we're in a new place,* we should be asking and relying on God for everything. When we're in a season of doubt or fear, it is prime time to proclaim the promises of God over ourselves and our families. When we don't know which way to turn, that's when we should be standing on every word of truth from Scripture: "Life and death are in the power of the tongue."[ii] So choose life! Pray! Worship! Encourage yourself with Scripture! Out loud! Even at the risk of looking crazy. We're taking new ground in full obedience to Christ. And like Esther, we too are on a mission.

3. *We can choose to believe God, like Mary.*

It's easy to get caught up in the world's noise, to put more stock in what other people say about us rather than what God says about us. I am guilty of this every day. Mary could have easily drowned in sorrow from harsh criticism and judgmental slander. But she chose to believe God. She chose to believe that what He spoke over her and what He put in her were true.

---

ii   Proverbs 18:21

God, help me to be like Mary. Help me to believe I am chosen, not forsaken. You are for me, not against me. You will never leave me. Even in an unknown land, You will provide for me and protect me. I am blessed and carry the Spirit of the Living God inside me.

With everything in me, I want to believe God. Don't you? Let's believe God together.

Stubborn obedience will undoubtedly lead you into new territories. And for me, obedience led me to a literal new country, 8,000 miles away from home. I had put feet to my faith.

Now it was time to do the next right thing.

Use my voice.

And choose to believe God.

chapter 7

A SINGLE, SOLITARY
Sermon

Our friend Kasadha Emma met us at the airport. I was eager to get to know this man who would be so instrumental in facilitating our adoption. I found out that Emma, though small in stature, was a giant in the kingdom of God. He was in his late 20's and newly married. His wife, Sarah, had just given birth to their first baby, a girl named Catrina. Along with being a registered nurse practitioner, Emma was continuing his studies to become a doctor. He was the founder of Care Medical Center in Kampala, a clinic offering medical care and counseling to women who found themselves with an unwanted pregnancy. He also started and pastored a church called Passion Christian Assembly. At roughly the same age, my life's accomplishments thus far felt completely inadequate when compared to Emma's achievements. I was honored to be in his company.

SWEET BABY JAMES

Our first order of business in Uganda was to meet our son, James. Emma drove us directly to the hospital in Kampala, where James was suffering with malaria. Never in a million years did I expect my first encounter with my new son would take place in a hospital room while he was fighting for his life.

I had been praying for this meeting. Months of waiting and planning and stressing had led me to this moment: seeing my child face-to-face for the first time. I would finally be able to hold him. To touch him. To embrace him. But I also knew this baby would have absolutely no clue who we were, and that Bradley and I would probably be the first white people (Mzungu) James had ever seen. I knew we were about to turn this baby's world upside down.

The hour-long drive from Entebbe airport to the medical center in Kampala felt like an eternity, but I tried to take in my surroundings. Winding roads cutting through a sea of red dirt. Children roaming freely, half-clothed and unattended. Women coming and going with large baskets perfectly balanced on top of their heads. Houses and huts made of clay. Vendors selling fresh flowers and bottled water at every corner. All of this would have fascinated me to no end had I not been laser focused on the little boy awaiting me at our destination. As it was, I happily accepted the slight distraction that these intriguing sites offered along our way.

The hospital was cold and sterile and uninviting, as most hospitals are. We wound our way through halls and up and down stairs, until we finally reached his room. And there, surrounded by nurses and attendants, was my son. My James.

He was beautiful. At nearly two years old, he was tiny with plump cheeks, dark eyes, and full lips. We approached him cautiously, hoping not to frighten him, though there was no wiping the smile off my face or hiding the tears threatening to spill down my cheeks. I was seeing the promise of God fulfilled with my own eyes. I was beholding the evidence of God's faithfulness. I was experiencing the goodness of God in the form of a little toddler.

James was sitting up in his bed, refusing the juice offered him by a nurse attempting to ward off dehydration. Much to my horror, he had an IV port *in his neck*. I had never seen anything like this but was told it was a customary practice when veins continue to collapse. Our eyes met. I saw an exhausted, ill, frightened little boy. I hope he saw love.

I was determined to win him over as quickly as possible. With the approval of the nurse, I presented a red lollipop from my bag and handed it over. James licked it and smiled. This gave me the courage to keep going. I held my hand out to him and he touched me with his soft, dimpled fingers. Sweet mercy. I whispered softly, "Hi James. I'm your new mommy. You don't know this yet, but I love you so much." I knew he didn't understand my English words, but I prayed he heard my heart. I loved this child.

Bradley sat on the other side of James and offered him a small toy I had packed in my bag. He took it without hesitation. With his eager acceptance of the lollipop and toy, I made an attempt at offering him some juice, which he drank. After a few minutes of quiet play, I motioned for him to sit in my lap. To my shock, he willingly crawled over, and nestled onto my lap, where we continued to work on taking sips of juice. These small victories might as well have been Olympic gold medals to us.

We were told the medicine given to James was successfully fighting his malaria symptoms, but he would need another day or so of monitoring before he could be discharged. We knew the best thing for him was to rest. And we needed rest after our travels, too. So with heavy hearts, we left him at the hospital in the care of the doctors and nurses, and continued on our way.

And then we got to our "hotel."

I don't know exactly what I had been expecting, but whatever my expectations may have been, I should have lowered them. The hotel was more like a hostel or a remote summer sleepaway camp. All the rooms had exterior entrances and were accessed by hiking up a dirt path from the lobby. This was easier said than done with our oversized luggage and trunks full of supplies. Once we hauled all our bags to our room, we attempted to settle in.

Our space was small, consisting of two twin beds featuring firm mattresses. Both beds were encapsulated by mosquito nets. A nightstand, and a tiny desk and chair completed the furnishings. Our bathroom was cramped, but adequate. Air conditioning didn't exist.

The depth of my exhaustion was indescribable. Bradley and I set an alarm to wake us up for dinner and each collapsed on a twin bed.

DIVINE DINNER

After we awakened, we walked down the dirt path to the dining room near the lobby. I expected to feel better after a nap, but instead, the magnitude of my situation became more clear. As I sat down to dinner, all my feelings started to catch up with me. The months of planning and stressing. The rush to pack up for our trip in five days. The overwhelming sadness of leaving my daughters behind in Texas. The twenty-six hours spent on a plane. The new country. The jetlag. Meeting our son in a hospital room, then leaving him there. The anticipation of meeting our yet unknown Ugandan daughter. The monstrous assignment ahead of us. So much work yet to accomplish. Still doubting God's plan. I saw the buildup of these feelings coming at me like a tidal wave. And I let it wash over me.

Bradley and I both sat at the table and sobbed.

I don't know how long we cried. I don't remember what we ate for dinner. But I will never forget the divine appointment awaiting us at this meal.

A Caucasian man sat down to eat at the table next to us. We exchanged initial greetings before each turning our attention to the meal in front of us. Bradley and I wiped away tears as we ate. The man noticed our obvious distress and engaged us in conversation.

His name was Errol Meaney. He was an evangelist from Australia, visiting Uganda to partner with a few ministries in the area. He was supposed to be preaching at a crusade that evening, but his transportation never showed up. Thus, he was stranded at our hotel and found himself eating dinner alone at a table next to us.

Errol asked us about our travels and why we were in Uganda. He was also clearly concerned about our apparent anguish. We invited him to sit with us and told him everything.

In his jovial Australian accent, he said, "I had a sermon prepared for the service tonight. Would you mind if I shared a little of it with you? Perhaps it will encourage you." We eagerly agreed. His sermon was based on Psalm 23:

> The Lord is my shepherd; I have what I need.
> He lets me lie down in green pastures; he leads
> me beside quiet waters.
> He renews my life; he leads me along the right
> paths for his name's sake.
> Even when I go through the darkest valley,
> I fear no danger, for you are with me;
> your rod and your staff—they comfort me.
> You prepare a table before me in the presence of
> my enemies;
> you anoint my head with oil; my cup overflows.
> Only goodness and faithful love will pursue me
> all the days of my life,
> and I will dwell in the house of the Lord as long
> as I live.

Errol focused on the word "through" in verse 4: "Even when I go *through* the darkest valley..." This word reminded us that our current situation was not permanent. God hadn't brought us here to leave us here, but to walk us *through* and to finish the task. Was our current valley dark? *Yes*. Were we lonely? *Yes*. Were we overwhelmed by the task ahead of us? *Yes*. Were we afraid? *Yes*.

But we were not without hope. Not only did we have the promise of God's presence with us, we also had the power of His protection. "I will fear no danger; for you are with me; your rod and your staff—they comfort me."[i] The rod and staff mentioned

---

i   Psalm 23:4

in this verse symbolize God's unfailing protection for His sheep as He guides them through the valley. The same rod that wards off our enemies provides safety for our souls. What a divine comfort.

While we may have found ourselves in the middle of a very dark valley, we could rest assured we weren't there to stay. God would bring us through it, His presence and protection guaranteed. He would absolutely finish what He started.

Tears streamed down our faces as Bradley and I listened to Errol's sermon. We knew it was no accident his transportation failed to show up that afternoon. We knew it was no coincidence this man of God happened to be sitting next to us at dinner that night. We knew this was a divine appointment. A providential moment. A gift from the Lord to assure us we were in the center of His plan. A reminder that we weren't forgotten. A blessed affirmation that God's presence would continue to be with us on our journey. We knew we were meant to be the sole audience of Errol's sermon that evening.

Even as I sit here and type this, my eyes well up with tears thinking about the faithfulness of God. Who are we that He would send a messenger from halfway around the world to meet with us in an obscure African hotel and deliver such a specific and profound word to us? With billions of people on this planet, all with tremendous problems of their own, God had His eye on me and cared so deeply about my distress that He sent a minister to encourage me—literally in the middle of nowhere. I can't help but recall the words to one of my favorites Psalms:

> Where can I go to escape your Spirit?
> Where can I flee from your presence?

> If I live at the eastern horizon
> or settle at the western limits,
> even there your hand will lead me;
> your right hand will hold on to me.
> (Psalm 139:7, 9-10)

Sweet Friend, you may find yourself in the middle of your own dark valley today. You may be completely overwhelmed with the assignment in front of you. There may be no visible end in sight. You may be doubting God's plan and purpose. You may be experiencing unimaginable pain. You may be questioning the Lord's goodness and faithfulness, unsure of His trustworthiness. If you'll allow me, I want to be a messenger of hope for you today. I'd like to minister to you the same way Errol ministered to me that night in Kampala, Uganda.

If we were together, I would sit across from you and grab both of your hands in mine and look you square in the eye. Listen to me carefully. Friend, God sees you. *(Yes, you.)* You have never, not even for a minute, escaped His notice. Even though you may not feel it, *His presence has never been closer.* I know this because Psalm 34:18 says, "The Lord is near to the brokenhearted; he saves those crushed in spirit." And I believe God's word is true. You can keep your chin up and place one foot in front of the other, knowing that even though you are currently in a dark valley, you have nothing to fear because God's presence is with you and He promises to protect you. Your present circumstance will not last forever. He didn't bring you to this valley to leave you here. God will bring you *through* it. He will complete what He began in you. He is stubbornly faithful to the finish. You are right where you're supposed to be. God hasn't made a mistake with you. He has never failed you, and He won't fail you any time soon. You can trust His plan.

If we were together, I'd hand you some tissues because we'd probably both be crying and mascara would undoubtedly be running down both of our beautiful faces. We'd hug, then I'd say something absurdly stupid to lighten up the mood a little. And I'd have you quote the Bible verse that you've surely memorized by now:

"He who calls you is faithful; he will surely do it."[ii]

And we would both know right now, in this moment, He is. And He will.

---

ii   1 Thessalonians 5:24

chapter 8

WHEN THE PROMISE
Rejects You

I woke up the morning after our Divine Dinner feeling refreshed and full of purpose. Emma came to the hotel early to pick me up and take me to the hospital to see James. Bradley stayed behind to work.

As I entered James' room, I could tell he recognized me from the day before. I pulled out yet another lollipop and handed it to him because I was willing to bribe for this child's affection with candy. We spent the morning hours playing with his toys, reading books, and looking at pictures on my phone.

Around lunchtime, the doctor came in to examine James. I was thrilled to hear he was being discharged! The nurse brought in a stack of papers for me to sign. Among them, a document declaring I had temporary legal custody.

We stopped by a pharmacy to pick up some medication on the way back to the hotel. I also grabbed a few grocery items including bottled water, juice, and fresh fruit. James was still exhausted and listless from the malaria, and I knew I would have to be diligent with his nutrition to help get his strength up. I hadn't told Bradley I would be bringing James back with me and was looking forward to surprising him. I'll never forget how my husband's face lit up when I walked into our hotel room carrying our sweet boy on my hip.

We spent the next hour or so playing with toys and reading books. I was able to get him to eat a few bananas and try a bite of my peanut butter and jelly sandwich, which he didn't love. I could see his eyelids start to get heavy and decided it was a good idea for both James and me to take a nap. I laid him in the bed next to me and gently rubbed his back until he gave in to sleep.

After waking up from our nap, we had a snack and Bradley took James outside to play catch with a ball we brought from Texas. James liked being outdoors and easily engaged in any physical activity. He was all boy and the newness of this little testosterone toddler thrilled us. But in the midst of all of this fun, James never once smiled. He didn't laugh. We could tell from his body language he was enjoying playing outside, but his face refused to communicate pleasure. James seemed to wear a deep sadness like an invisible robe. Even while having a good time, he carried a gloom.

The rest of that first day continued in an uneventful manner. And then it was bedtime.

It was after we had given James a bath and put him in his new pajamas that he decided he didn't want to stay with us any longer. He had spent a fun day with these new white people and was ready to go back to a familiar place, which definitely was not our hotel room. He let us know he was finished with us by marching over to the door to our room and planting himself there with his back towards us, as if waiting for someone to open the door for him so he could leave. We tried multiple tactics to coax him into coming to bed: books, toys, snacks, you name it. But

James didn't budge. This defiant display was amusing at first, until we realized his sincerity. This baby boy had no plans of staying with us.

At this exact moment, my computer began ringing with an incoming Skype call. My mother had made it to Dallas and was united with my daughters back home. I clicked "answer" and I saw all their smiling faces on my screen: my mom, who had sacrificed so much to come stay with my kids; Ava, who knew where I was and what I was doing, and was so proud of our mission; Greta, who was cheering me on with her big blue eyes and gap-toothed grin; Harper, who had no clue what was going on, but was just thrilled to see her mommy on the computer screen. I saw people who loved me, who knew that I loved them. I saw people who missed me, who wanted to be with me. I saw my family.

And at the front door of our hotel room, a million miles from our home, there stood my little boy who wanted absolutely nothing to do with me. A boy about whom God had spoken to me so clearly. A boy for whom I had worked tirelessly for months and months. A boy for whom I had abandoned all that was comfortable. A boy for whom I left behind all my family. This boy was rejecting me. He was unknowingly breaking my heart. The juxtaposition of the boy in my room who didn't want anything to do with me and the girls on my screen from the other end of the world who missed me like crazy was more than I could handle. And I fell apart.

It was an ugly, snotty cry, filled with heaving sobs and gasps for air. And my girls back in Texas witnessed it all via Skype. Definitely not my finest moment.

I attempted to compose myself. The girls' new little brother was in our room, and they wanted to be introduced. But James was still by the door. I walked over and gently picked him up and carried him to the computer. He sat listless in my lap, lacking any emotion. Ava, Greta, and Harper lit up at the sight of their new brother in my arms. They took turns introducing themselves and telling funny jokes and making silly faces to try to get James to smile. But his face remained expressionless.

After a few minutes of catching up, we turned off Skype and closed the computer. James wiggled out of my arms and returned to the door. He stubbornly had not abandoned his mission. He still wanted to leave. This time, I didn't try to get him to move. I didn't try to change his mind. Instead, I joined him. I walked over and sat next to him. Instead of asking anything of him, I merely offered my company. He was afraid and in pain. And so, I sat with him.

I don't remember how long we stayed by the door. Could've been five minutes. Could've been an hour. But I do remember that the baby boy eventually got tired and climbed into my lap. I gently carried him over to the bed and fell asleep next to him.

Bradley and I had undeniably been called by God to adopt James. We were on a very clear mission. He left no room for doubt. God had given us the promise that two precious Ugandan children would be added to our family. I had imagined many different scenarios involving our first day with James, but having him attempt to leave us never occurred to me as an option. We never dreamed that our promise wouldn't want us.

What do you do when your promise rejects you?

What do you do when the person or the place or the thing

that God has promised to you seemingly denies you? What do you do when things don't pan out the way you expected? What do you do when something you've been praying for happens to crush your spirit? What do you do? What did we do?

We returned to the promise God gave us, we dug in our heels, and we stubbornly stood on it.

Just like Abraham.

God made an unbreakable promise to Abraham, a covenant regarding his offspring, that they would be as numerous as the stars in the sky. The problem? Abraham was 100 years old and his wife, Sarah, was 90. A little long in the tooth for childbearing. But, of course, God delivered on His word and Sarah gave birth to Isaac, the promised son. This child would be the catalyst God would use to make Abraham "the father of many nations." God was very specific with His vow:

> But God said, "Your wife Sarah will bear you a son, and you will name him Isaac. I will confirm my covenant with him as a permanent covenant for his future offspring." (Genesis 17:19)

God left no doubt of His plans for Abraham's son, Isaac, so it's absolutely baffling that He would ask Abraham to sacrifice Isaac on Mount Moriah just a few short chapters later in Genesis 22. This child, this son of the covenant, was the channel through which God would populate the earth with Abraham's descendants. How did Abraham respond to God seemingly taking away that which was promised?

Abraham didn't flinch. He dug his heels in and stubbornly believed his God—the God of the Covenant. He knew it was impossible for God to go back on His word, even when all earthly evidence seemed to indicate otherwise. Abraham believed God would provide a substitutionary sacrifice, or even if he killed Isaac, God would raise him from the dead. Either way, Isaac would live, and God's word would stand. Because God's word *always* stands.

At just the right moment, God provided a substitutionary sacrifice so Isaac could live. A wildly majestic foreshadowing of the Sacrificial Lamb who would pay the ultimate price so you and I could live. The Perfect Substitute who was crucified on the altar of our sins was God's own beloved Son, Jesus. God gave Abraham a glimpse of His glory on Mount Moriah that day.

Friend, here's the good news for both of us. The same God who was faithful to keep His promise to Abraham is the same God who is faithful to keep His promise to me and you today. Even when all indications seem to say otherwise, God's word to us will hold fast. His promises stand forever. He is unable to break a vow. His covenant is secure.

So when it seems like God's plan is falling through, or you're disappointed with how things are falling into place, go back to His promises. When you find yourself in a foreign land and the thing He's promised you seems to be rejecting you, go back to His covenant. Go back to the thing He called you to do. Go back to His Word. Grab hold of it and white-knuckle it with all you have. Hold onto it for dear life. Dig your heels in and believe your God—the God of the Covenant. The God of Abraham, Isaac, and Jacob. The God who is the same yesterday, today, and forever. This God is *your* God. And "He who calls you is faithful; he will surely do it."[i] (I had to remind you again.)

A SPECIAL WORD FOR POTENTIAL ADOPTIVE PARENTS

I want to take a minute and talk to you, sweet adoptive Mom, about what it can be like to meet your baby for the first time. Having been an adoptive mother for over nine years to date, I now know that the events of our first day with James were to be expected and I should have been prepared for rejection. But I didn't know this then.

Nobody warned me.

I was more focused on *my* needs and *my* expectations, rather than on the earth-shattering transitions James was experiencing. For starters, he had just been discharged from the hospital after a severe bout with malaria. That's traumatizing in and of itself. His body was not fully healed. Then, he was removed from the family who had been caring for him and placed in the custody of two people with bizarre-looking white skin. We looked nothing like anybody he had ever encountered. We smelled different. We felt different. Our language was different. On top of that, we brought him to a hotel room he'd never seen and fed him foods foreign to him. (Hello, PB&J?!) Nothing was familiar to this child. He experienced a fight-or-flight reaction. His body's natural response was to attempt to run away from us.

And I took it personally.

I interpreted James' fear as rejection. I made the mistake of inserting myself as the center of the universe in this moment,

---

i   1 Thessalonians 5:24

rather than focusing on the trauma engulfing my son.

Every adoption is unique and special in its own way. There is no "One Size Fits All" approach to this thing. Everybody's story will be different. Many adoptions take place at birth, placing a newborn baby in their second parents' arms. And this is a precious thing. But some of you may be adopting older babies, toddlers, or children. If this is the case for you, please know this: while you have been dying to meet this child (for months or even years), your child has most likely not been dying to meet you. If you're adopting a baby over the age of one year, please align your expectations with the reality of your situation: you are a stranger to this child. And can I take it a step further?

This child owes you nothing.

This may be a tough pill to swallow, but it's necessary to hear. As much as you've been aching to hug and kiss this baby, your first meeting is most likely not the time for intimate physical touch. This is a privilege that has to be earned through multiple deposits of trust and felt safety. If your child is a different ethnicity than you, please be aware you may be the first of your race with whom your child has ever been exposed. The color of your skin may be an anomaly to your new son or daughter. The food you eat may be foreign. The scent of your perfume may be too strong. Your language may be new. Your laugh may be too loud. The air conditioning in your house may be too cold.

And all of this is okay.

There is so much *newness* for everyone involved, including you. And God's grace abounds for all of it. Things won't be perfect on Day One. They probably won't be perfect on Day 101, either. Because there are no perfect days. There are only grace-filled moments. It takes time to bond with your new child. It takes time to connect as a family unit. Give yourself and your child the gift of time and be kind to yourself along the way. Be patient with yourself and with your child. Keep your expectations realistic. Keep your focus on your child's needs rather than your emotions. Keep your trust in God's unfailing grace.[ii]

And be prepared to behold the transformative power of love.

---

ii   See Appendix for Adoption Resources

chapter 9

I BLESS THE RAINS DOWN
in Africa

We took the next step of our journey the following morning, which involved the first of many road trips across the Ugandan landscape. James was from a village in far east Uganda, near the Kenya border, and it was necessary to travel there to collect essential paperwork and documents. Emma showed up at our hotel early in the morning to pick us up. Accompanying him was our Ugandan attorney, George, who was overseeing the legal procedures of our adoption. George was nothing like Emma. Emma was compassionate, gentle, ready to laugh, full of life. George was blunt, critical, dry, to the point. George was a grouch.

Bradley, James, and I climbed into the back seat of Emma's SUV. A hallmark attribute of the Ugandan culture: very little details are given. Ever. About anything. We were in the dark as to exactly where we were going or how long it would take us to get there or exactly what we would be doing when we arrived. We were on assignment in a foreign country with no other choice but to trust Emma and George. So, we got in the car and settled in for the ride from Kampala to God Knows Where.

Here's some wisdom for you, Friend. When you find yourself in a foreign country or a new territory, link arms with those who have experienced it before. People who have been there and done that. Those who have insight into your situation and understand the language, customs, and culture of where God is calling you. If you're a new mom, seek out older moms and glean from their discernment and perspective. If God is calling you to start a new business, find other people who have successfully done the same and learn from them. If God is calling you to write, sing, paint, teach, preach, or build, then make it a habit of becoming a student of those who have experience in your field. Know when to submit yourself to the authority of wise counsel. Know when to be quiet and follow an expert's leadership. Know when to get in the back seat of the car and trust that God has put a great team of helpers around you. "Take good counsel and accept correction—that's the way to live wisely and well."[i]

I've mentioned that air conditioning didn't exist at our hotel. It didn't exist in Emma's SUV, either. And I quickly discovered that in Uganda, children's car seats were also nonexistent. These were happy exemptions for me. The lack of air conditioning meant my window stayed down to provide a breeze, which gave me a front-row seat to the gorgeous African terrain. The lack of car seat meant James sat in my lap the entire trip, which gave us both time to bond and become familiar with one another. On this day, the absence of familiar American conveniences was a blessing.

We drove for hours, stopping only to eat lunch at a roadside restaurant, gas up the car, and stretch our legs. We made it to the bustling town of Mbale, which I incorrectly assumed would be our destination. Turns out, we were heading for the mountains to

---

i   Proverbs 19:20 MSG

a remote village not found on a map: Muzetati.

As we turned onto the isolated red dirt road that would lead us into the hills, Emma quietly stated, "It's raining in Kenya." And sure enough, up ahead, a storm was visible. The distant sky had grown dark and heavy and was releasing its angst on the fertile slopes of the countryside. I wasn't aware of our close proximity to Kenya and found it fascinating we had driven far enough to see another country. Another foreign place that I'd yet to experience. Another people group beloved by God. Another landscape full of divine beauty. Emma's follow-up comment seemed ominous: "I hope it doesn't come this way."

By the time we reached Muzetati, the storm had arrived from Kenya. The sky opened up and delivered a deluge unlike anything I had ever seen. The rain was hard and fast. I quickly raised my window to keep from getting soaked. I could see small rivers forming in the cracks and crannies of the red dirt road that sliced through the village. The wind whirled and rocked us back and forth; branches, leaves, and garbage were blowing by Emma's car. We pulled over and parked next to a small hut. It was decided we would sit in our car until the downpour passed.

A few minutes into our storm-induced stall came an occurrence I will never forget. I began to hear a loud male voice over some sort of intercom system, passionately shouting in a language unbeknownst to me. I wiped the fog off my window and scanned the village. Not too far from us, a man was standing in the bed of a truck, speaking into a portable sound system with heartfelt intensity. And all around, people slowly began emerging from their various shelters and walking toward the truck, as if drawn in by a magnet. In the middle of the pouring rain. With no care or concern for the water rushing around them. Before long, a crowd of nearly 100 people stood around the truck, mesmerized by the fiery message being delivered. I couldn't imagine any kind of speech that would induce me to stand ankle-deep in red mud while being barraged by an onslaught of precipitation.

And that's when Emma, with his quiet confidence, made the statement that will mark me for the rest of my life:

"They are hungry for the gospel."

I can still hear his Ugandan accent as he said it. So off-the-cuff. So matter-of-fact. And that single sentence cut me to my core. I know what it feels like to be exceptionally hungry for good news.

Can I take a quick break from adoption storytelling for a bit? Can I bring you back to present-day Texas to hang out with me for a while? I'm sitting here in my cozy bed writing this chapter about an experience I had nine years ago in Africa, and I'm currently living through my own desperate situation in real time.

Three weeks ago, I found a large lump in my right breast, about the size of a grape. I'm 38 years old. Lumps in my breast are not something I'd ever considered as an option. Or at least not an option for this early in my life. I took the first available appointment my gynecologist had to offer, which happened to be three days ago. Meaning, I waited for two whole weeks between finding the lump and seeing a medical professional. Do you know the depths of the psychological trauma you can inflict on yourself in two weeks' time? My brain tends to go to the absolute worst-case scenario in exactly 0.0023 seconds, which involves me losing my hair, enduring multiple rounds of chemo, and eventually writing my obituary. But then my faith kicks in and I'm convinced that I'm whole and I'm healthy and I will live and not die and I still have decades left and all is well. The mental gymnastics are mind-boggling.

Receiving bad news from the doctor is not a new phenomenon for me. My dad was first diagnosed with a malignant brain tumor when I was 16 years old. I watched him endure chemotherapy, radiation, tests, surgeries, and procedures of all kinds until the Lord called him home in 2018 at the age of 59. He wrestled with cancer for 20 years. My dad rarely received good reports from his doctor appointments. My years of experience with him had given me the framework to anticipate disappointing news. I was expecting history to repeat itself with me.

After two weeks of freaking out, I was surprisingly calm when I entered my gynecologist's office three days ago. But my serenity quickly evaporated. As she was examining my right breast, her eyes widened and she stated, "This lump shouldn't be there." To which I quietly responded, "I know."

I was instructed to put my clothes back on, and by the time I was fully dressed, my doctor returned and simply said, "Follow me." She walked me to her private office, where she had the radiologist's assistant waiting on the phone to collect my insurance information. I had a mammogram scheduled for the following morning at 8:00 AM. We were wasting no time.

The haste of my doctor's actions sent me into a downward spiral. Up until this point, the lump was an enigma. A secret. Something I could explain away because it wasn't quantifiable. But a professional medical examination removed all ambiguity. There was a definite mass. My gynecologist felt it. It shouldn't be there. And an immediate mammogram was scheduled.

I was a single rider on my very own emotional rollercoaster for the remainder of that day. I felt a heaviness in my chest. Breathing became difficult. My entire body was on high alert. Sleep alluded me that night. My mind led me down another doomsday tailspin.

I was up bright and early the next day to make the 30-minute drive to the radiologist's office. I listened to a random podcast in the car to take my mind off the morning's impending events, because sometimes there's nothing like other peoples' drama to help you forget your own. As I checked in with the nurse, I was told I would be receiving my results from the mammogram immediately. This was a relief. I didn't know how much longer I could wait for answers.

This was my very first mammogram. At my age, I assumed I had a few more years to go before being subjected to the boob torture chamber. I had heard nothing but horror stories about how painful this procedure was, which added to my overall panic surrounding the day.

The mammogram was not comfortable, but it was quick. Thank God. I was then ushered into another waiting room where I was informed the doctor wanted additional images of my right breast and had ordered an ultrasound. This was not part of the original plan. I was expecting to have a mammogram with immediate answers, not more waiting and more tests. My anxiety was through the roof.

After sitting in the waiting area for what felt like an hour, I was led into a small, dark room filled with ultrasound equipment. The stenographer made swift work of my scans, focusing mainly on my right breast. She could see my lumpy intruder on her screen and measured it from every angle. My breast ached as she moved it around and manipulated it to get the perfect images. My mind was racing. My heart was pounding. I had to remind myself to breathe as absolute despair was settling in.

The stenographer stood up and let me know the doctor would be in soon with the results of my mammogram and ultrasound. And I continued preparing myself for horrible news. After the events of the previous 24 hours, I had lost all hope. The seriousness of my situation had become clear, and fear had permeated every part of my being. I thought about how Bradley would react. I thought about how I was going to break the news to my children. I found myself ankle-deep in mud, my own personal storm raging around me. My anguish was palpable.

A few minutes went by before the door opened and the doctor walked in. I could feel every muscle in my body tense up. I was ready for the sucker punch.

She didn't bother with any kind of greeting or polite formalities. She looked me dead in the eye and got right to the point.

"I have good news for you."

She kept talking, but I didn't hear anything else beyond that sentence. No other words were required. I heaved a deep sob and the tears started flowing. She had good news for me. I don't have cancer. I'm not sick. I'm not dying. My body is healthy. I'm going to be okay. My husband will still have a wife. My children will still have a mother. This was incredible news.

(If you're a worrier like I am, I'll go ahead and put your mind at ease. I was diagnosed with a fibroadenoma cyst, which is completely harmless and is brought about by weight gain, stress, and elevated caffeine intake. All of which I'm 100% guilty. Because I have 5 kids and I love food. Being skinny and well-rested is not my testimony.)

Friend, I don't believe it's a coincidence God allowed me to experience this health scare while writing this chapter. He gave me a very visceral understanding of what it means to be desperate for good news, just as the villagers were hungry for the gospel on that rainy day in Muzetati. When you don't have Jesus, what hope do you have? What purpose do you have? What peace, joy, and love do you have? The apostle Paul said it best: "For in him we live and move and have our being."[ii] I never want to lose sight of the utter starvation my soul would experience without the Lord. I want to stay hungry for His presence in my life. Because He stays ready to satisfy my every need.

There's an amazing account recorded in the New Testament about a woman who was desperate for a touch from Jesus. Let's look at her story found in Mark 5:25-34:

> Now a woman suffering from bleeding for twelve years had endured much under many doctors. She had spent everything she had and was not helped at all. On the contrary, she became worse. Having heard about Jesus, she came up behind him in the crowd and touched his clothing. For she said, "If I just touch his clothes, I'll be made well." Instantly her flow of blood ceased, and she sensed in her body that she was healed of

---

ii   Acts 17:24

her affliction. At once Jesus realized in himself that power had gone out from him. He turned around in the crowd and said, "Who touched my clothes?" His disciples said to him, "You see the crowd pressing against you, and yet you say, 'Who touched me?'" But he was looking around to see who had done this. The woman, with fear and trembling, knowing what had happened to her, came and fell down before him, and told him the whole truth. "Daughter," he said to her, "your faith has saved you. Go in peace and be healed from your affliction."

This woman was acutely aware of her need for Jesus. She had endured over a decade of pain and suffering. She tried everything else, exhausting all other resources and possibilities. She had nothing left to lose. With the little strength she could muster, she was able to push through the stifling mob engulfing Jesus and briefly brush the hem of His jacket. Even amidst the crowd pressing in on Him, Jesus felt the exchanging of her hunger for His healing. Her desperate faith received His divine focus.

That rainy day in Muzetati left its mark on me. I will never get over the image of hundreds of villagers standing in a storm to hear Good News. I now understand their desperation.

My prayer for myself and for you is that we will never be satisfied with the trappings of this life. May we never become content with our modern-day conveniences and our Comfortable Christianity that we forget our very next heartbeat is a gift from Almighty God. May we forever be aware of our frailty and our nothingness apart from His breath in our lungs. May we always be hungry for the presence of our Heavenly Father. So much so that we're willing to stubbornly push through hardships, difficulties, and roadblocks to grab hold of His garment. That we will be content with nothing less than an encounter with Jesus. His presence is the only satisfaction to the hunger of our hearts. Even if it means standing in the rain.

chapter 10

Once the storm passed, it was time to get down to the business at hand: collecting essential paperwork and documents for James' court date. A gentleman by the name of Issah joined us in Muzetati. He was the district Probation Officer in charge of overseeing the welfare of the orphans within the community. He hopped in Emma's SUV along with Bradley, James, our attorney, George, and me as we continued along the red dirt road to track down local officials who could help facilitate our mission. It was during this car ride that I was given the full account of James' story:

It began with a peasant woman named Halai Agatha. Agatha was married to a man named Michael and was the mother of eight children. As a Muslim, Michael had multiple wives and dozens of children; therefore, the burden fell on Agatha to provide and care for her children. During my time in Uganda, I discovered Agatha's story is not uncommon. Roughly 14% of the country's population practices Islam, with over 8% of women in Uganda involved in a polygamous relationship.[3] I observed firsthand the fortitude of Ugandan women. Many are the sole income-earners for their household. They start small businesses and work multiple jobs. They are single-handedly providing for their families, raising their kids, and caring for loved ones. The women of Uganda are proud. They are strong. They are courageous. They are resilient. They are a beautiful marvel to behold.

One day, Agatha journeyed outside of her village in search of food she could gather for her children. The terrain of eastern Uganda is bountiful and lush. The persistent rain and fertile soil yield a wonderful harvest, with the primary crops being coffee, tea, sugar, plantains, corn, cassava, and sweet potatoes.[4] I frequently witnessed children walking along Ugandan streets nibbling on fresh sugar cane they had cut from the shrubs themselves. The coffee is out of this world. The fruit is fresh and vibrantly sweet. The rich, red dirt is one of Uganda's most treasured assets. Agatha's search for food took her into a thicket along the border of Uganda and Kenya. It was there, while gathering crops, she heard a sound so wildly unexpected: the cry of a baby.

She began to search for the source of this sound, listening intently as all thoughts of her harvest instantly evaporated. After a few minutes of combing the landscape, she found him. *Under a coffee bush.* A baby boy, totally alone and naked other than the cloth that loosely wrapped him. He appeared to be less than six months old, as he was unable to crawl or walk. Agatha immediately scooped up the child and began looking around for who could've left him unattended. Finding no one else within the area, she made the trek back to her home in Muzetati.

The baby was not welcomed at her house. As far as her husband was concerned, this child was just another body on a very long list of mouths to feed, all of whom he already couldn't afford to support. Agatha was ordered to take the infant to the village orphanage, called a "baby home," and leave him there.

Agatha attempted to comply with this mandate, but the baby home was at full capacity and could not accept any more children. This is yet another typical scenario in Uganda: There are more orphans than caretakers to provide for them. She had no other option but to take the child back to her home. Agatha named the baby Mumwata James.

But the baby was still not welcomed. And now, because of her disobedience, Agatha was not welcomed, either. Agatha, Mumwata, and all eight of her children were thrown out of their home and onto the streets. Michael was done with all of them. To her credit, Agatha went straight to the authorities and reported her situation. The police swiftly got involved and demanded Michael allow his family to return home.

This launched an investigation into the origin of the lost baby. Multiple district officials, magistrates, and agents got involved with the search for this child's family, all in an attempt to get answers to significant questions:

- Where was this baby from?
- Who are his parents?
- Where is his family?

- Are they searching for him?
- Was he brought across the border from Kenya?
- Was there any criminal activity involved?
- Is his mother in danger?

This quest for information lasted almost a full year and yielded absolutely zero results. Meanwhile, Mumwata remained in Agatha's care. Despite the disdain of her husband, she lovingly provided him with shelter, food, and protection. She treated him the same as the rest of her children, caring for him to the best of her ability. The overall climate of the home, however, remained hostile, due to Michael's animosity. Agatha was openly defying her husband's wishes by keeping this lost baby under her roof, offering him precious resources that should've been allotted to the other children.

Our new friend Issah was heavily involved in the investigation surrounding Mumwata. He became acquainted with Kasadha Emma, who came to his district from Kampala on a medical mission trip. Emma's expertise is medicine; his anointing is evangelism. He fulfills both to the glory of God. While on this medical ministry trip, Emma heard about the baby named Mumwata James who had been found under a coffee bush, with no known family, living in a hostile environment because the orphanage was full. Emma happened to be helping a family from Texas with their adoption process at this exact same time, who had yet to be matched with a baby boy. He began inquiring with Issah and the other local officials as to the possibility of an international adoption for Mumwata. With no known red flags or roadblocks, Emma, along with the district officers, helped match this lost boy with the Knight family from Dallas, TX.

As with many children in Uganda, when they get sick there is a scarcity of funds to pay for medication, which contributes to chronic, untreated illnesses. Rampant malnutrition inhibits their little bodies from fighting any kind of virus. This keeps them in a pattern of poor health. The cycle is vicious. And it makes the medical ministry Emma provides all the more valuable. So, when Mumwata contracted malaria, his prospects for healthcare in Muzetati were very grim. Emma was contacted for assistance and was given permission to take Mumwata back to Kampala for more comprehensive treatment. The baby was admitted to the hospital where he received proper care to combat the malaria ravaging his little body. It was there that he met a white couple who had journeyed all the way from Plano, TX, because God had given them clear instruction and wide-open doors. And they were stubborn enough to obey Him.

I listened to Issah's account of my son's story, enraptured at the hand of God in all of it: His timing, His attention to detail, His perfect plan for this lost baby, and how Bradley and I were miraculously included in God's grand scheme. I felt humbled and small, in awe of the greatness of my Savior. His lovingkindness made me want to weep with gratitude.

THE POWER OF A NAME

During our entire adoption process, I had this uneasy feeling in the pit of my stomach whenever our son was referred to as "Mumwata." I couldn't quite put my finger on it, but I didn't like it at all. When I learned that his full name was "Mumwata James," I was both relieved and thrilled because James is a family name (my mother's maiden name). And "James Knight" had a classy ring to it. I immediately began calling him "James" since I was unable to shake the apprehension I felt every time I heard the name "Mumwata." I figured we would have the opportunity to change his full name once we fully adopted him, so I didn't give much weight to my feelings. However, during this car ride I discovered what the name "Mumwata" means in Luganda, his native language.

Mumwata is Lugandan for "dumped, trash, thrown out, abandoned."

In Uganda, names are very significant. Jennifer Ostrowski best explains the Ugandan tradition of naming children:

> Rather than receiving given names and surnames at birth, most Ugandans receive religious names and clan names. Each family member receives his or her own individual clan name. As a result, a mother, father, and their children do not share a single name but have different names all associated with the same clan. When a Ugandan hears a clan name, they are able to associate that name with a certain clan, or with the region where a given clan comes from. Yet, unlike surnames,

clan names are frequently used like given names or first names. Ester Masane can just as easily be called Masane Ester. As a result, if I were to greet her, I could say either, "Hello, Masane!" or "Hello, Ester!" While religious names can be selected by any family member, or even close friends, clan names are almost always chosen by a child's paternal grandfather. Children are sometimes named according to a favorite proverb, the season of their birth, or birth order.[5]

Agatha gave the lost baby the religious name of James. But because there was no known paternal grandfather to bestow him with a clan name, the task landed in her lap. She chose the name "Mumwata," which described how she found him: *Garbage. Forsaken. Junk.*

And this was the name that my precious child was called every day of his life, for months on end.

"Mumwata" was the first word he heard directed his way as his brain and cognitive functions were developing during his crucial first two years of life. "Mumwata" was the name to which he responded when called. "Mumwata" was the name that formed his identity. "Mumwata" was the word he heard from adults and children alike. "Mumwata" was the only existence he knew.

This revelation crushed me. It tore my heart out of my chest. And I'm still not fully recovered, to be honest. I don't understand how anybody could speak that word over a child. Yes, I realize there are native customs and traditions in every country and I will always honor and value my children's African heritage. And even though it's something I'm immensely proud of, I'll never fully comprehend the Ugandan way of life. I understand there are centuries-long practices with naming children, and it won't all make sense to me.

But how can anyone name a baby "trash?"

Christopher Giovagnoni recently wrote an article for Compassion International and he hit the nail on the head:

> Names have significance. They have power. They define us. They're more than a bunch of letters grouped together to sound pleasant to the ear. Names are more than a convenience allowing people to talk to each other. Names are a gift from God. These words contain His power. They give things meaning. They bring us meaning.[6]

Solomon shares this wisdom with us in Proverbs 22:1: "A good name is to be chosen over great wealth; favor is better than silver and gold."

Names carry significance. I learned a lot more than James' history in the car with Issah that day. I learned that God had His hand of protection on him from his very first breath. I learned that God ordered Agatha's steps while searching for food on that divine day near the Kenya border. I learned that Agatha truly had a mother's heart to go to such lengths to protect and provide for James, even at the risk of her own safety. I learned God providentially connected Issah and Emma through medical ministry, which supernaturally led us to unite with a beautiful little Ugandan boy. And I learned that, come hell or high water, I would be changing my son's name.

chapter 11

MZUNGU *Mommy*

We continued our trek through the countryside in and around the village of Muzetati, tracking down various government officials and agents, procuring necessary documents and paperwork for our first court appearance. Our son's story was somewhat notorious, and many of the locals came around to get a good look at the Mzungu (white) couple who were adopting James.

I don't think I fully understood how weighty this excursion to Muzetati would be. I was expecting it to be a joyride through the Ugandan landscape, collecting forms and records along the way, seeing the sites, meeting new people. And while this was somewhat true, there was a heaviness that settled on me throughout the events of the day. Observing the villagers' determination to hear the gospel in the pouring rain was intense. Learning the details of James' story was heartbreaking. Witnessing the abject poverty that engulfed the beautiful people of Muzetati was painful. The scope of need around me was overwhelming. The realization of my smallness and helplessness was exhausting.

But the most difficult part of my day came that evening, when we met Halai Agatha, the woman who found James under the coffee bush.

True to Ugandan form, I had not been told beforehand that we would be meeting Agatha. Not that it would've changed anything. There was no warning that could've possibly prepared me for this meeting. Having literally just heard the full story that day, I had so many unprocessed thoughts and emotions regarding this courageous woman.

Agatha met us in Muzetati and planned to join us for dinner back in the town of Mbale. As she climbed into Emma's (crowded!) SUV, I was able to observe her. She had a small frame and her hair was cropped short against her head, as is the style of many Ugandan women. She wore a modest blue dress and a pair of worn-out shoes. She was shy and demure, barely able to make eye contact with me. I gave her the warmest greeting I could possibly give, my heart so full of gratitude towards her.

And then James saw Agatha.

He literally jumped out of my arms and climbed over Bradley to embrace her. The woman who found him. The woman who took him into her home and fed him. The woman who was willing to defy her husband in order to protect him. The woman who provided for him though resources were scarce. This woman was the only mother James had known up to this point in his life. I watched her cling to him. My son. She hugged him and held him in such a familiar, natural way. They obviously knew each other well.

I was instantly jealous. And I was instantly devastated.

I was jealous because Agatha had a bond with my son I didn't yet have. They had history together. They had shared experiences. They had intimate knowledge of one another. They spoke the same language. They appeared to belong together. She looked like his mother. And he looked like her child.

I was devastated because I was going to be the one responsible for separating them. I would be forcing James to leave the only home he knew, however hostile and volatile it may have been. I would be taking a child from a woman who had sacrificed so much in order to shield and safeguard his life. Agatha faced the wrath of her husband in order to take this baby into her home. And I was now taking him away from her. I was also devastated because I didn't look like either of them. My skin wasn't dark. I was an outsider. I was the Mzungu mommy. I would be teaching this Ugandan boy a new language, new customs, and new traditions. James would never look like he belonged with me. And I would never look like I belonged with him. And it wrecked me.

James sat in Agatha's lap throughout dinner. She fed him. She knew exactly what foods he liked, how to cut his meat in a specific way, and how to let him peel his own banana. They played pat-a-cake games with their hands, as if they'd done so a thousand times before. I quietly sat and observed it all. The language barrier made conversation with Agatha difficult, so we didn't engage in much dialogue. As it was, I was too physically and emotionally exhausted by the events of the day to put forth much effort. And she seemed more comfortable and content to eat her food and play with my son in her lap.

After dinner, we said our goodbyes. We would be driving back to Kampala through the night, and Agatha and Issah planned to catch a bus back to Muzetati. When it was time to load the car, I quietly told Emma, "You need to take James from Agatha's arms. I can't do it." He nodded his head as if he understood while I climbed into the back seat of the car. Through the window, I watched the scene unfold.

Agatha saw Emma coming towards her and clung to James with all her might. She didn't turn her back or try to walk away, but she tightened her grip. And James reciprocated. He hugged her back just as tightly. Emma whispered something to Agatha, and gently took James from her arms. I could see tears running down her cheeks as James began to scream and reach for her. He was wailing as Emma brought him to the car and placed him in my lap. James fell against my chest and continued to cry uncontrollably for the next two hours. I let him. And I cried with him.

The pain James felt when Emma took him from Agatha was visceral. It was deep and it was intense. It's a pain I'll never know or fully comprehend. The agony of being pulled away from the only mother you've known, only to be thrust into the arms of a white mother you barely know, is nothing short of traumatizing. To experience yet another life-altering transition at such a young age was just another devastating wound for him to suffer. And my hands caused the suffering.

THE COST OF STUBBORN OBEDIENCE

I've wrestled with this for many years now, and I want to wade into these murky waters with you, Friend, if you'll join me. I want you and I to grapple with this question (because it's absolutely worth the effort): *What do you do when your stubborn obedience causes someone else to suffer?*

How do you move forward in surrender and submission when the thing God has called you to do inflicts pain on another? Do you trust Him? Do you believe His plan is good for everyone involved? Even if you never witness the good with your own eyes? Do you obey Him at all costs?

There's a fascinating story recorded in the gospel of Luke about an African man named Simon of Cyrene and the role he played in the crucifixion of Jesus. He's only mentioned in one verse; a "blink and you miss it" narrative: "As they led him [Jesus] away, they seized Simon, a Cyrenian, who was coming in from the country, and laid the cross on him to carry behind Jesus."[i]

In the history of mankind, there has never been another human more stubbornly obedient than Jesus Christ: "he humbled himself by becoming obedient to the point of death—even to death on a cross."[ii] And here, in this one verse found in Luke 23:26, we see a small glimpse of how Jesus' radical obedience caused an African man to suffer.

Based on clues found in Scripture, we can surmise Simon was coming to Jerusalem from Libya to worship during the Festival of Unleavened Bread. He was minding his own business on this dark Friday that Christianity has since deemed "Good," when he came face to face with the man whose bleeding flesh embodied the ultimate unleavened bread. Simon must have been tired from his journey, ready to rest his aching feet or find a cool drink of water from a nearby well, when he stumbled across the Via Dolorosa, "The Road of Suffering," unaware that the

---

i   Luke 23:26
ii   Philippians 2:4

punishment his sin deserved was being inflicted on this innocent Jewish man before his very eyes. Simon could not have known.

But he would suffer.

Out of the multitude gathered that day, Simon was chosen to carry Jesus' heavy cross up the hill to Golgotha. It was Simon who had to stoop down low and lift the heavy wooden beam from the shoulders of the man who would save his soul. It was Simon, with his sore feet and aching back and intense thirst, who would look Jesus in the eye as He felt the weight of God's holiness and displeasure with our sin. It was Simon who would feel Jesus' blood drip off the cross and onto his skin, not knowing that just one drop would cleanse him for eternity. It was Simon who would watch as Jesus was nailed to the plank he had just carried and then hung between two thieves. It was Simon who would hear Jesus say, "Father, forgive them, because they do not know what they are doing."[iii]   It was Simon who would be the first to demonstrate the principle of sacrificial obedience Jesus had taught the disciples just a few chapters earlier in the book of Luke: "Then he said to them all, 'If anyone wants to follow after me, let him deny himself, take up his cross daily, and follow me.'"[iv]

Jesus' obedience to the cross carried a cost for Simon of Cyrene, just as our obedience to Jesus will carry a cost for those around us. Because following Jesus is costly.

Can we trust God enough to let Him handle the hurt and pain our obedience inflicts on others? Can I trust God enough to believe His plan for Agatha is good, even though my obedience

---

iii   Luke 23:24
iv   Luke 9:23

caused her to suffer? Can I believe God has a marvelous purpose for James' life as part of the Knight family, even if taking him away from Agatha caused him grief? Can we really trust God with the suffering that accompanies obedience?

Simon of Cyrene would say, "Heck yes." (Probably.)

Tradition tells us that after the crucifixion, Simon stayed in Jerusalem with the disciples and was possibly even in the upper room on the Day of Pentecost, when the Holy Spirit was given. (Oh, to have been there!!!) He is mentioned in the gospel accounts of Matthew, Mark, and Luke, which tells us he was well-known among the disciples. His sons, Rufus and Alexander, were saved and became evangelists. Simon is even credited with taking the gospel back to the continent of Africa. All due to the pain he suffered because of Jesus' obedience to the cross on that Good Friday. Simon's suffering worked out for his good and for God's glory.

Oswald Chambers' masterful pen encourages us: "If we obey God, he will care for those who have suffered the consequences of our obedience. We must simply obey, and leave all the consequences to him."[7]

That's it in a nutshell. We obey. God handles the consequences. For everyone involved. We're not all-knowing or ever-present or all-powerful. But God is. He knows the beginning from the end, in all situations, for all people, always. He is stubbornly faithful, so we have no other choice but to be stubbornly obedient. Even if it causes pain to those around us. His divine purpose redeemed the suffering of an African man on assignment in Jerusalem thousands of years ago, just as His providential plan healed the heart of a certain Mzungu Mommy fulfilling her calling in Uganda, stubbornly obeying the Lord at all costs. He is faithful. He's big enough to handle all of it.

So trust Him to handle it.

chapter 12

My Help

The day after our journey to Muzetati was Sunday, our first Sunday in Uganda. Emma invited us to join him for services at the church he founded, Passion Christian Assembly. We eagerly accepted. Oh, how I needed the refreshment that comes from corporate worship and sound biblical teaching. After the emotionally tumultuous week I had just experienced, I was ready to sit and soak in the Word.

Emma picked us up early that morning, dressed in his Sunday best. Bradley and I hadn't packed dressy clothes, so we wore what we had. On the way to church, Emma dropped a bomb on me: "Holly, I would love for you to preach the sermon today."

My head whipped around and my eyebrows shot up. "Me? Not Bradley?"

Emma assured me I was the one for the job that day. His congregation was mostly women who had come to Christ through the ministry of Care Medical Center, his pro-life clinic, and it would bless them to hear from a woman who was strong in her faith. I agreed to preach and immediately began praying God would give me words to say, as I literally had nothing prepared and church started in less than an hour. But Emma had yet another request: "Will you also sing for us? Do you know 'My Help' by The Brooklyn Tabernacle Choir?"

Did I know "My Help" by The Brooklyn Tabernacle Choir? Um. Yes. Yes, I did.

"My Help" is one of my favorite songs of all time. It is lyrically a straight lift from Psalm 121. It is in my bones. I grew up on The Brooklyn Tabernacle Choir. I listened to all their albums and watched all their videos. I heard "My Help" for the first time when I was in 8th grade and just knew the song was mine to sing. And because my dad was the worship pastor at our church, I just knew he'd ask me to sing it with our choir. *But he asked my mom to sing it instead.* Fast forward a few years. Bradley and I were married and serving at our church in Dallas. "My Help" was pulled out of the archives for our choir to sing. And because I was one of the featured soloists at our church, I just knew I'd get asked to lead that song with the choir. After all, that song was in my heart. I knew it backwards and forwards. I had loved it since the 8th grade. *But someone else was asked to sing it instead.*

Yes. I knew "My Help." It was the song that was never meant to be for me.

Until this beautiful Sunday in Kampala, Uganda.

The song was mine to sing on this day. I wasn't on a grand stage with bright lights and smoke and lyrics on a screen. I wasn't in my typical slick black attire and full makeup. There was no fancy sound system to amplify my voice. No band or orchestra or choir. There weren't thousands of people in the congregation.

This day was much sweeter.

Instead of a grand stage, I stood on a dirt floor in an open-air room filled with folding chairs. Instead of my stage clothes, I wore a t-shirt, long cotton skirt, and flip flops. Instead of a fancy sound system, Emma played a CD track on a boombox. Instead of a band, choir, or orchestra, my precious husband sat nearby, harmonizing with me on the chorus, and my darling James stood at my side, grasping onto my leg as I sang. Instead of thousands of congregants, there were dozens of Ugandan women I didn't know, all with different stories, most of them survivors of deep pain, trauma, and abandonment. Many sat there nursing their babies at their breast. Babies they had, at one point, considered aborting. But they chose life. And now they were looking at me to minister to them.

What a heavy calling.

It was my honor to sing these lyrics, straight from Scripture. Let them wash over you today, Friend:

> I will lift up mine eyes to the hills
> From whence cometh my help.
> My help cometh from the Lord,
> The Lord which made heaven and earth.
> He said he will not suffer thy foot,
> Thy foot to be moved.
> The Lord which keepeth thee,
> He will not slumber nor sleep.
> Oh, the Lord is thy keeper,
> The Lord is thy shade
> Upon thy right hand, upon thy right hand.
> No, the sun shall not smite thee by day,
> Nor the moon by night.

He shall preserve thy soul even forevermore.
My help, my help, my help
All of my help cometh from the Lord.[8]

The Lord had ordained this song, for this day, for my voice, for this audience. He knew what He was doing all along. He knew that withholding the opportunity to sing in front of thousands would make it that much holier to sing in front of dozens. Even as I sang over the ladies, tears fell down my cheeks as I felt the weight of the truth of this song. The God who protects me and helps me in all my trouble is the same God who protects these beautiful women and helps them in all of their distress. These words apply to everybody, everywhere, all the time. God is that big.

Do you want to hear something cool? My story with "My Help" didn't end in Uganda. In 2016, God called Bradley and me to move to New York City to serve in the music ministry *at the actual Brooklyn Tabernacle.* (As in, we moved our family of seven from Texas to New York City. It was as wheels-off as you might imagine. But that's another book for another day.) I was honored to sing with The Brooklyn Tabernacle Choir for four years, until God called us back to Dallas during the Covid pandemic. The first time we sang "My Help," I stood in that choir loft surrounded by hundreds of angelic voices in awe of the faithfulness of God. He had brought me full circle with this beloved song. I didn't sing the solo. And I didn't want to. I had experienced that song on just about every level imaginable, including with the actual choir who recorded it. And that dirt floor in Uganda will always remain my favorite.

OUR EYES ARE ON YOU

It was on that same dirt floor in Uganda that I had to preach my very first sermon.

I had been struggling with what to preach from the moment Emma asked. I felt so helpless. So inadequate. So insufficient. These precious ladies had been through hell and back. Some had been raped and abandoned. Others, like Agatha, were one of multiple wives to the same man. Many were solely responsible for earning income and providing for their children. Some didn't know where their next meal would come from. Almost all of them were entrenched in unseen battles, fighting for their families.

What in the world could I possibly have to say to these women?

And then it hit me. *I have absolutely nothing to say.* There were literally no words I could possibly give to these women that could help them in any way.

But God is never at a loss for words.

As it turns out, He had plenty to say. All I had to do was open my Bible and let His word speak for me and through me. I turned to one of my favorite passages, 2 Chronicles 20. In this chapter, the army of Judah was completely surrounded by enemies on all sides. King Jehoshaphat "resolved to seek the Lord and proclaimed a fast for all of Judah" (v.3). He then stood among the vast assembly and prayed one of my favorite prayers recorded in Scripture. It's my favorite because Jehoshaphat got super bold with his approach to God. Jehoshaphat said:

Lord, God of our ancestors, are you not the God

who is in heaven, and do you not rule over all the
kingdoms of the nations? Power and might are in
your hand, and no one can stand against you. Are
you not our God who drove out the inhabitants of
this land before your people Israel and who gave
it forever to the descendants of Abraham your
friend? They have lived in the land and have built
you a sanctuary in it for your name and have said,
"If disaster comes on us—sword or judgment,
pestilence or famine—we will stand before this
temple and before you, for your name is in this
temple. We will cry out to you because of our
destress and you will hear and deliver."
(2 Chronicles 20:6-9)

Do you see why I love this prayer? I picture Jehoshaphat
pointing his finger at God, passionately reminding Him of His
faithfulness and His power and His might and His greatness. I
imagine he's saying to God, *Don't you remember who you are?*
Don't you remember how you've come through for us in the
past? You've got to come through for us again! Your covenant
with Abraham is on the line! Your name is at stake!

A few verses down, Jehoshaphat famously said, "We do not
know what to do, but we look to you" (v.12). Like the psalmist,
their eyes were lifted to the hills, from whence cometh their
help. They had no other choice in the matter. They were pinned
in from every side. The only direction they could look was up.
He was their only help. If God didn't show up, the story would
be over.

But, of course, God showed up.

2 Chron 20:12

He showed up in the form of a prophetic word given to one of the Levites, which was the worshiping-leading tribe. (I've always loved that part.) The word?

> Do not be afraid or discouraged because of this vast number, for the battle is not yours, but God's... You do not have to fight this battle. Position yourselves, stand still, and see the salvation of the Lord. (2 Chronicles 20:15, 17a)

God instructed the Israelites to dress for battle, stand their ground, and shout their praises. When they did this, the Lord set an ambush against their enemies, and they defeated each other. Nobody escaped. God delivered a victory to the Israelites that day. He was all the help they needed. He made a way where there was no way. And all they had to do was stand and worship Him.

That's the message God had for my own heart and the women of Passion Christian Assembly, as I preached my very first sermon on that dirt floor in Kampala, Uganda. I didn't have to be brilliant or eloquent. I simply had to point them to the Source of their help. I watched as their eyes lit up with understanding and they nodded their heads in agreement. As I led them in a chorus at the end of my sermon, I watched as they closed their eyes and sang, hands raised in the air.

They were ready for battle.

And this message is for you too, Friend. This Truth is universal. It's true for the single mom in Africa. It's true for the retired grandmother in Alabama. It's true for the college student in Oregon. It's true for me. It's true for my children.

When you find yourself pressed on every side, surrounded by darkness, and you don't know what to do, lift your sweet head and fix your eyes on your Helper. Remind Him of His faithfulness to you. Remind Him of His promises to your family. Remind Him of His power and might and greatness. Praise Him for the victory you already have because His very name is Victory and you are His child. It very well may be that this battle is not yours to fight. Position yourself, stand firm on His word, praise His holy name, and see the salvation of the Lord. How do you do this?

- *Position yourself.* Dress for battle by putting on the full armor of God: the belt of truth, the breastplate of righteousness, the shield of faith, the helmet of salvation, and the sword of the Spirit.[i] You'll notice that the only offensive weapon is the sword of the Spirit, which signifies the Word of God. All other pieces of armor are used for defensive purpose. In other words, gird yourself with truth, righteousness, and faith, and you'll be well-equipped to hold your ground.

- *Stand firm.* Plant both of your dainty feet squarely on the firm foundation of Scripture and don't budge. Grab hold of every promise that belongs to you in God's Holy Word and white-knuckle it like your life depends on it. Because it does.

- *Praise the Lord.* Your worship confounds the enemy. He becomes disoriented when we praise the Lord in the midst of our trials. And because God inhabits our praises, our worship ushers His presence into our battles, where

---

i   Ephesians 6:14-15

He delivers the victory. So turn that worship music on full blast, sing at the top of your lungs, and let the enemy have it.

- *See the salvation of the Lord.* Your eyes have to be open in order to see Him. Just like Jehoshaphat prayed: "We don't know what to do, but our eyes are on you."[ii] Just like the psalmist said: "I will lift up mine eyes to the hills from whence cometh my help."[iii]

Get dressed for battle, even if it's not your Sunday best. Stand firm on God's promises, even if it's on a dirt floor. Sing your praises, even if there's no one around. And see the salvation of the Lord. Open your eyes, Friend, and fix them on the One who is your ever-present Help in time of trouble.

---

ii   2 Chronicles 2:12
iii   Psalm 121:1

chapter 13

THAT'S MY *Daughter*

At this point, we had been in Uganda for a full week. It was time to meet the baby girl who would become my fourth daughter: Akansasira Joan. Unlike the trek to Muzetati for James, we knew exactly where we were going and how long we'd be there. Joan was in an orphanage in the southwestern corner, near the border of Rwanda—on the complete opposite end of the country. This meant we had a 12-hour drive ahead of us. And we would be gone for five days.

The usual suspects piled back into the trusty SUV: Emma in the driver's seat, our attorney George in the passenger seat, and Bradley, James, and me in the back row. Windows down and worship music blaring, we settled in for the journey.

Oh, the beautiful landscape we beheld. Tree covered hills, verdant valleys, crystal clear lakes, rich red dirt. We witnessed women walking barefoot along the side of the highway, proudly carrying humongous baskets and bushels on top of their heads, as if they were weightless. We saw men riding bicycles with entire sofas strapped onto the back. We observed students in their pristine uniforms making their way to their respective schoolhouses. In every village we drove through, we caught a glimpse of small children playing together, nearly always unattended. I soaked in everything I saw, taking mental pictures, attempting to remember every detail. I was slowly but surely falling in love with the country of Uganda.

A few hours into our drive, Emma pulled the car over without warning and told us to get out. As I looked around, I realized he had stopped at the equator. Yes, the *actual equator*. We had our picture taken straddling the line, each leg in a different hemisphere. We felt like we were at the center of the world. Bradley (of course) paid the money to watch the toilets flush in opposite directions, just a few feet apart. He was ridiculously fascinated by this. I bought a lovely coffee table book at the gift shop nearby before loading back into the car.

Our road trip continued on, uneventful. We made a few stops along the way for gas and food, eventually making it to the town of Kabale by nightfall. The sky was velvety black as we pulled into the White Horse Inn, where we would be staying for the week. Our room was nice, with two queen beds and a large garden tub, perfect for bathing our active little toddler. A full day in an SUV driving along bumpy Ugandan roads had left our bodies exhausted. All three of us collapsed into our beds and fell soundly asleep.

I awoke the next morning full of expectation. This was the day I would be meeting my daughter! I quickly got myself and James dressed for the day before making our way to the hotel's restaurant for breakfast with Bradley, Emma, and George. As we left our room and stepped out into the morning light, I couldn't believe my eyes. Our hotel seemed to be sitting on top of a mountain, overlooking the town of Kabale below us, blanketed in misty fog. The green grass surrounding the hotel was thick and vibrant. The flower beds were immaculately landscaped. The hotel itself was an elegant brick structure, with multiple steeples and spires, resembling an African castle. There was a playground in a small field adjacent to the restaurant, begging James to come play. I felt like I had awakened in a dream. I whispered a sincere "thank you, Lord" under my breath as we entered the dining room.

While we ate, Emma and George prepared us for the day's events. We would be driving from Kabale to the town of Kisoro, which was another two-hour drive through the mountains to our west. (So. Much. Driving.) There, we would briefly visit the orphanage, meet Joan, and devise a strategy with the orphanage administrators to obtain the few forms still missing from her file. With this plan in place, we assumed our positions in Emma's SUV.

Having grown up in Colorado, I was familiar with mountainous terrains and winding roads, but I was speechless as we drove through the dense forest blanketing these Ugandan peaks. Emma told us tall tales of people getting lost in these mountains, never to be found again. At one point, he quietly said, "Keep your eyes open for gorillas." *Say what?* Turns out we were near Mgahinga Gorilla National Park. I immediately began praying we wouldn't crash or run out of gas. Today was not my day to be lunch for a primate. I needed to make it off this mountain in one piece.

We arrived in Kisoro, and as we drove through the gate to the orphanage, I was instantly taken with the picturesque setting. If I haven't described it enough already, the Ugandan landscape is absolutely gorgeous. The orphanage was nestled at the base of a mountain, a compound of white clay buildings with green tile roofs, surrounded by a white wooden fence. Palm trees swayed in the breeze that brought with it the scent of freshly cut grass.

We parked the SUV and were met by a tall, lanky woman with her hair cropped short against her head. She introduced herself as Annette, Joan's social worker. Behind her was a gentleman with a kind disposition, a few wrinkles on his face, and some gray hair at his temples. His name was Ezra, and he served as the senior administrator of the orphanage. Annette quickly went over a few details regarding Joan but would save the bulk of her story for later. Apparently, Joan was around 23 months old and had recently been "upgraded" to the toddler room because she had started to walk. This timeline didn't add up to me, but there was no time to ponder it or ask questions. To the toddler room we marched, Annette leading the way.

Bradley held James as he and I stood back, away from the entrance to the small white building with the green roof that housed the toddlers. While Annette spoke with the woman in charge, I snuck a peek of the room. Inside, there were babies everywhere. Some playing on the floor with toys, some feeding themselves bowls of porridge, some crying for assistance, some napping on cots. The mass pandemonium of a room full of toddlers.

Another worker appeared, seemingly out of nowhere, with a baby on her hip. One glimpse of this child and I lost my breath. My heart stopped beating. My stomach flipped. I got chills. And in the core of my soul, I knew.

That's my daughter.

The baby was thrust into my arms. She took one wide-eyed look at me, and immediately began screaming. I took a good look at her and inhaled her stench and I wanted to start crying, too. Other than a flimsy hand-me-down shirt, Joan was naked and covered in urine. No pants, no diaper. Nothing. I was later told that diapers were too expensive to keep on every baby at the orphanage, so many are forced to stay covered in their own filth. Joan's face was dirty from the remnants of the porridge she had attempted to feed herself. It was caked onto her shirt and stuck in the crevices of her neck. Her belly was painfully enormous. Her eyes were swollen from crying. Both of her ears were excreting white puss, the smell of which was nauseating and alarming. And all I could think was, *My God, I love her.*

I loved her so much it hurt.

The reaction I had to this precious child was physically intense. I ached for her. I longed for her to be healthy and well and whole and happy. And I knew I would do whatever necessary within my power to make this happen. Because she was my daughter.

I got so caught up with her I forgot about Bradley and James. They needed to meet Joan, too. Bradley and I switched babies and I watched him gently hold our baby girl, speaking softly to her.

The two of us standing there, in the middle of Africa, holding our two little Ugandan children, it all felt so right. It felt divine. It felt good. We were holding the promises of God in our very hands, staring into their beautiful brown eyes. We knew we were exactly where we were meant to be. I was seeing the goodness of God in the land of the living. I felt like I could exhale.

All too soon, Annette took Joan out of Bradley's arms and returned her to the toddler room. Our next mission involved traveling to Joan's village to retrieve paperwork from local officials, while she remained at the orphanage. I felt as if my heart was torn out of my body and stayed back at the orphanage with her.

Walking back to the car, I was overwhelmed with emotion. And, quite honestly, I was a bit confused. I was dumbfounded at the visceral response I had when meeting Joan, yet I didn't have those same feelings when I met James. Or even when I met my biological daughters, for that matter. Why did I react so strongly to Joan? *Why her?*

Looking back, I believe on that divine day at the orphanage in Kisoro, God gave me a glimpse of how He feels about me. Just like Joan, I was covered in filth when God found me. My sin had left me dirty, foul, unclean. The stench of my transgressions was strong. I, too, had failed at feeding myself, at caring for myself. I, too, was naked and ashamed. My mind needed healing. My soul needed nourishment. The tears needed to be wiped from my eyes. My ears longed for the sound of a Gentle Voice. Like Joan, I was a mess.

And God, in His outrageous lovingkindness, looked at me and said *That's my daughter.*

He didn't expect me to clean myself up before He was willing to embrace me. He didn't ask me to get my life together or figure it out before He accepted me. He loved me, just as I was.

He loves you, too, Friend. Just as you are.

And it's a physical, visceral, painful love. A love so strong that God was willing to sacrifice His only son to call you (*yes, you*) His daughter. A love so wild that it will chase after you. You can't run from it. Don't believe me? Romans 8:38-39 is pretty conclusive:

> For I am persuaded that neither death nor life, nor angels nor rulers, nor things present nor things to come, nor powers, nor height nor depth, nor any other created thing will be able to separate us from the love of God that is in Christ Jesus our Lord.

Still not convinced? Let's look at Ephesians 3:17b-19:

> I pray that you, being rooted and firmly established in love, may be able to comprehend with all the saints what is the length and width, height and depth of God's love, and to know Christ's love that surpasses knowledge, so that you may be filled with all the fullness of God.

You may be in a season of life where you're questioning God's love for you. You may have bought into the lie that nobody cares for you. You may feel dirty or shamed by a secret sin. You may be struggling with temptation no one knows about and no one sees. But God sees you. He sees all of you—your regret, your guilt, your pain, your loneliness, your struggle. And He adores you.

Sweet friend, if it's been a while since you've felt loved or cherished, please accept this chapter as a love letter to you straight from your Father. Let His arms wrap around you. Feel

His delight in you. You don't have to clean yourself up. You don't have to get your life together. You don't have to figure everything out. He's already done all of that for you. Your only job is to be still and receive His embrace. Accept His grace, mercy, and healing. Abide in His love. And tune your ear to hear His gentle voice tenderly say to you:

That's my daughter.

chapter 14

FIFTEEN MILES PAST THE
Middle of Nowhere

Emma's SUV was getting crowded. Annette piled into the back row with Bradley, James and me, and we began a trek—quite literally—up the side of a mountain. Our destination? The small village of Rutaka, about 15 miles from the orphanage in Kisoro. Our mission? Locate Joan's grandfather, her only known adult relative, and obtain his signature on a few required forms for her file. Our transportation? Jam-packed.

I don't think it's fair to call the path we drove on up the mountain a road. It was not a road. It was more like a narrow dirt ledge on the side of a cliff without a single rail or safeguard in sight. We passed a few cars on their way down into town, and let me tell you, my cheeks were clinched. I immediately began to dread our return drive back to Kisoro. On the way up, we were on the inside "lane," against the mountain. On the way down, we would be on the suicide side. Kamikaze ridge. Death by landslide. Bradley and I held our breath for most of the two-hour drive up to Rutaka.

On the other hand, not a single Ugandan in our car seemed bothered or concerned about our treacherous trip in the slightest. In fact, Annette never stopped talking. I asked her to give me the details regarding Joan's first few months of life. Her words began pouring out. And she never came up for air.

I learned Joan had been born in a mud hut in Rutaka and her mother died a few weeks after childbirth from tuberculosis. Her father fled the country shortly thereafter, leaving Joan and an older sister, around the age of 10, in the care of their grandfather Peter, who had a well-known drinking problem. When it became apparent Peter had neither the desire nor the means to care for his granddaughters, Joan's sister stepped in and made an adult decision. She single-handedly carried Joan on her back 15 miles down that mountain from Rutaka to the orphanage in Kisoro.

I was not told until sometime later that Joan's sister was offered a job working at the orphanage and was there the day that we met her. My one and only regret in this entire adoption process is that I did not meet her precious sister and, at the very least, get a picture of her with Joan. God knows, had I met her, I probably would've attempted to move heaven and earth to adopt her, too. My attempts to locate her since then have turned out to be futile. I pray for this sweet girl every time I think of her. I don't even know her name. But God does. He sees her. And He loves her.

The orphanage took Joan into their care under the condition she would return to Rutaka at the age of two. They were strictly a "baby home" and did not have the space to care for children past this age.

It was at this point I raised my questions regarding Joan's age. When I met Joan earlier that day, Annette told me she was 23 months old, had just begun walking, and had therefore been promoted to the toddler room. As a mother who was actively raising three little girls, this math didn't add up to me. Babies generally begin walking around 12 months old, not 23 months old. Of course, every baby is different and some may have developmental delays, but I had held Joan in my arms. Albeit briefly, I had looked her over and examined her. Other than the obvious nutritional concerns and infected ears, she did not seem to have any developmental or growth delays. By all appearances, and in my experience as a mother of small children, she seemed to be roughly 12-14 months old, *not* 23 months old.

"Are you certain Joan is really 23 months old?" I asked.

"Of course not," was Annette's reply.

Most babies are not born in hospitals in Uganda, and therefore their births are not properly documented. The orphanage based Joan's age on dates and details given to them by her sister, regardless of their validity. This was all the information they had to work with.

"So you're telling me Joan would be sent back to Rutaka next month to fend for herself if we weren't here to adopt her?" was my next question.

"Mmmmm." Annette's Ugandan affirmation.

I sat there in the crowded SUV and processed everything I was being told. As with James' story, the timing of Joan's situation was nothing short of miraculous. The Lord sent us to Uganda at the exact moment necessary to adopt this baby girl— just before she was to be sent back to her village and cared for by God-knows-who.

Only God could orchestrate something so grand, yet so specific.

SNOW WHITE

From the driver's seat, Emma announced that we had arrived at Rutaka. I looked out the window and observed my surroundings. Rutaka made James' village of Muzetati look like a bustling metropolis. From the center of town, I counted exactly eight buildings, including a small schoolhouse constructed of mud. Emma parked the car and he, George, and Annette set out to inquire as to the whereabouts of Joan's grandfather, Peter.

Bradley, James, and I got out of the car to stretch our legs and look around. The size of the town and its distance from all other civilization became glaringly evident to me. Rutaka can't be found on a map. As the remoteness of our location began to sink into my psyche, I said out loud: "If we die here, nobody will ever find us."

And I wasn't wrong. We were 15 miles past the middle of nowhere.

Before long, villagers began to emerge to catch a glimpse of the Mzungu (white people). Without a doubt, we were probably the first Mzungu most of them had ever seen. The adults stayed back and openly talked about us in their native language. But the children came right up to us. Their courage was rewarded with smiles and lollipops from my backpack.

I'll never forget one particular little girl. She was beautiful. Probably around the age of six, and she was wearing, of all things, a dirty, tattered Snow White princess dress. Bradley noticed her, too. And he verbalized my thoughts: "How does a Snow White dress make it all the way to Rutaka, Uganda?" Where did it come from? How did it get here? Does this darling child even know who Snow White is?

I watched her lick her lollipop and spin around in her dress, proud of the way the skirt ballooned as she twirled. Her innocent, natural femininity reminded me of my three little girls back in Texas. And the isolation of our current location washed over me, yet again. The realization of the distance between me and my children back home nearly knocked me over. What I wouldn't give to be with my daughters and watch them spin and twirl in their princess dresses at that very moment. To hear them laugh and giggle and sing. We were worlds apart. In the tree-covered mountains of Uganda, I felt invisible.

GOD SEES ME

Throughout this journey, I learned this lesson over and over again: The road of stubborn obedience is often accompanied by seasons of solitude and isolation. We see examples of this truth over and over in the Bible. Moses met with God alone on Mount Sinai. David was alone in the fields, shepherding his flock. Daniel was alone in a den filled with lions. Paul was alone in prison when he penned several of his epistles. John was exiled to the isle of Patmos, alone when he received the revelation of Jesus.

But the most tender illustration of this principle, in my opinion, is Hagar's story, found in Genesis 16. Hagar was an Egyptian slave, who served Abraham's wife, Sarah. (Do you remember these two? We met them a few chapters back when Abraham was commanded to sacrifice their son, Isaac.) The relationship between these two women was volatile, marked by jealousy, bitterness, and contempt. Sarah was unable to bear children, so she gave Hagar to her husband in order to build a family. When Sarah's plan actually worked and Hagar became pregnant with Abraham's child, Sarah lost her mind. She was overtaken by envy and resentment and mistreated Hagar so much so that Hagar ran away. Hagar found herself pregnant and alone in a wilderness. The cause of her isolation? Obedience to her master.

The Lord found Hagar in the wilderness. He met her in her solitude. He spoke gently to her and gave her instruction and direction. He blessed her and the son she was carrying. He gave her a purpose and a future. It was in her isolation Hagar originated one of my favorite names of God: El-Roi, "the God who sees me." This slave girl, pregnant with her master's baby, wandering alone in the wilderness, was never outside of God's sight. Hagar's obedience to her owner led her on a desolate path, where she was seen by God, met by God, and blessed by God.

God saw me on that mountain in Uganda that day. He knew where I was and what I was doing. He knew I was lonely. He knew I felt helpless. He knew I was being obedient to my Master, even though it hurt. God saw those precious children in Rutaka that day, too. He saw the beautiful girl twirl in her dress and enjoy a lollipop. He saw Emma, George, and Annette as they were helping us with all our paperwork. He saw my daughters back in Texas, too, as they went about their day, with their parents on the opposite end of the globe. He saw it all.

And He sees you, too, Friend. Right where you are. You may be going through your own season of isolation and solitude. You may be following the Lord, striving to obey His commands, submitting to the plan He has for you. Yet you find yourself in a lonely situation. It may be a physical place or an emotional wilderness. *Please hear me when I say, God sees you.* His name is Jehovah El-roi, The God Who Sees, and He cannot go against His nature. You can rest assured that you have never, not even for a minute, been outside of His sight. His attention is fixed on you. Psalm 17:8 says you are the "apple of God's eye." You are valuable. You are cherished. You are essential. You are seen.

Not only does God see you in your solitude, but He is with you. Just like He was with Hagar in the wilderness. Just like He was with me in Rutaka. This same God declared our Savior's name to be Emmanuel, "God With Us." He cannot go against His nature. Jesus told us with His own lips, "I am with you always, to the end of the age."[i] And we're promised that He will never leave us nor forsake us.[ii] We have this encouragement from Joshua 1:9.

> Be strong and courageous. Do not be afraid or discouraged, for the Lord your God is with you wherever you go.

His presence in our isolation is a guarantee. Which means we're never actually alone. We have the Creator of the universe by our side. We may feel lonely, but our feelings aren't always reliable. In her book, *Uninvited,* Lysa TerKeurst correctly states that "Feelings should be indicators, not dictators."[9] It may seem as if we're invisible, but this feeling doesn't align with the truth of Scripture.

When you're in a lonely place, you can be assured God sees

---

i   Matthew 28:20
ii   Hebrews 13:15

you and He is with you. You can also count on the fact that your obedience will bring a blessing, even in your isolation. During Hagar's wilderness experience, God saw her, He met with her, and He blessed her. God's name is El-Shaddai, "God Almighty," the God who is all-sufficient and all-bountiful, the source of all blessings. And He cannot go against His nature. Deuteronomy 5:33 gives us a mandate attached to a blessing.

> Follow the whole instruction the Lord your God has commanded you, so that you may live, prosper, and have a long life in the land you will possess.

Obedience is always accompanied by blessing. Even if it leads us first to a wilderness.

Sweet Friend, the next time you find yourself 15 miles past the middle of nowhere, my prayer is that you're filled with hope and courage. I pray you're able to combat your feelings of isolation with the rock solid truth that God knows right where you are. And being smack-dab in the middle of His will, even if you're all by yourself, is the safest place to be. May you be encouraged in knowing God sees you, God is with you, and God is eager to bless you. And may you be able to echo the words of Hagar found in Genesis 16:13: "Surely I have seen the One who sees me."

chapter 15

A FLASH OF *Favor*

Emma, George, and Annette found Joan's grandfather, Peter, bellied up to the bar at the local watering hole in Rutaka, stone cold drunk in the middle of the day. He was summoned to the town square, where he would meet the Mzungu couple who were attempting to adopt his granddaughter. We could see him stumbling towards us from a mile away. He was tall and slender, with a weathered face and a bald head. He wore a dark green, collared shirt that was unbuttoned lower than was necessary, with khaki pants tucked into rain boots.

Introductions were made and Peter went into a slurred diatribe in his native language. Annette, never at a loss for words, began engaging in dialogue with him, their voices raising above each other's. Neither one of them would let the other finish a sentence. Hands were flying, fingers were pointing, and brows were furrowed. It was a passionate exchange. I looked wide-eyed at Emma and asked, "What is going on?"

"Peter has many grandchildren. He wants you to adopt all of them and take them back to America with you," was his quiet reply.

This comment ripped my heart out. It was so complex.

On the one hand, I would be *thrilled* to adopt all these children who need a home! I saw the vast need all around me and ached to help every child in some way. On the other hand, God only called us to adopt *two*. And truly, I couldn't adopt every orphan in Uganda, as much as it killed me. It was an impossibility.

How was I supposed to respond to that?

Thankfully, I didn't have to. Annette responded for me. In Luganda. I have no idea what she said, but whatever it was, it was effective and ended the conversation quickly.

Peter eagerly signed all the paperwork presented to him and agreed to appear at Joan's court date at the end of the week. He was gracious in allowing us to take photos of him to have for Joan's sake. I was thankful for the opportunity to meet a blood relative of Joan, knowing this would be important to her as she grew older.

After our brief and colorful exchange with Peter, it was time for us to head back down the mountain to Kisoro. We had to return to the orphanage to tie up some loose ends with our paperwork before making our way back to our hotel in Kabale. There were still many miles to drive before the sun went down. We crammed into Emma's SUV and I mentally prepared myself for the treacherous trip down the cliffside road. Seatbelt buckled. Prayers offered. Booty clinched.

When we arrived at the orphanage (Alive! In one piece! Thank you, Jesus!), Ezra, the senior administrator, was waiting for us at the gate. Emma slowed the car and rolled down this window. Ezra began speaking in his native language, and Emma, George, and Annette all quickly began chiming in. Another pensive conversation took place right in front of us, not one word of which I understood. But I could read their body language. And it made my heart drop.

Something was wrong.

The conversation wrapped up and Emma parked the SUV on a patch of red dirt in front of the administrative offices. From the passenger seat, George turned around and said, "Do not get out of the car. Wait here until I call for you." And he walked into the main office, alone.

I begged Emma to fill me in: "Why was the air just sucked out of the car? Why did everyone seem concerned? What was the problem?"

Apparently, the founder and director of the orphanage was a British woman by the name of Jenny. She had been out of the country "on holiday" for the past few months and had just returned *that afternoon*, while we were in Rutaka. Ezra had been the one handling our adoption of Joan from the beginning. This was the first time Jenny had heard about the American couple seeking to adopt one of her orphans. *And she was livid.* Jenny, an adoptive mother herself, did not believe in allowing children to leave Uganda. She was a proponent of in-country adoption only, which I understood and would fully support, if only there were Ugandan families lined up to take in these children. But there weren't. I had witnessed the incredible need with my own eyes.

From inside the car, we could hear the voices of George and Jenny as they discussed our situation in her office. It sounded as if Jenny was doing most of the talking. George chimed in here and there. Words were difficult to make out.

After about 15 minutes, George appeared and waved his hand for us to join him. Emma and Annette accompanied

Bradley, James, and me into a large conference room filled with approximately nine orphanage workers. There were two chairs at the end of the room where we sat, facing them all. I said a quick prayer as I took my place. It felt as if we were on the witness stand.

Ezra began by making introductions for everybody in attendance. And then Jenny initiated our trial, hammering us with questions.

- What are your intentions?
- Why Uganda?
- Why would you ever want to take children out of their country and raise them as Americans?
- Don't you know how difficult it is to deal with adopted children?
- How will these children ever know about their heritage as Africans?
- The judge you will see for her case is difficult. He rarely grants guardianships.
- Why are you doing this?

As is the theme of our marriage, Bradley let me handle most of the talking. With sweet James sitting in my lap, I answered every question as honestly and authentically as I possibly could. I told them the story of God calling us to adopt and His clear confirmation of the country of Uganda. That we were following Him in obedience. That we believed God had a plan for both Joan and James and He had placed them in our family. That we were prepared to walk through whatever challenges may come our way. That we would honor their Ugandan heritage to the very best of our abilities. That we were trusting God to see us through this entire process. That we had three happy daughters at home we missed greatly. That we loved each other and loved the Lord. That this was *God's* plan. Not ours.

I finished speaking and held Jenny's gaze. She narrowed her eyes, tilted her head, and had the most miraculous momentary personality shift I've ever observed. Her features softened, her hands unfolded, and Jenny opened her mouth and kindly said, "Well, then. You better go get Joan and take her with you. She needs to get used to you before your court date."

Just like that.

God had given us a divine flash of favor with this woman. There's no other way to describe it. Ezra hopped up from his chair and brought us a small stack of papers to sign, one of which stated that we now had temporary legal custody of Joan. We shook hands with all the orphanage workers and left the office to find our daughter.

A woman was waiting for us outside, holding a freshly bathed, diapered, and clothed Joan in her arms. When she was handed to me this time around, she remembered who I was and didn't cry when I held her. Her ears, however, were still excreting puss and smelled horrific. I was eager to get her the medicine she so desperately needed. We made arrangements for Annette and Ezra to attend Joan's court date at the end of the week, and then we loaded up the SUV for the drive back to the White Horse Inn in Kabale.

FINDING HER VOICE

There were now two adults and two babies in the back seat of Emma's SUV—one in each of our laps. I was beyond exhausted from the events of the day and had mentally prepared myself to go through another disastrous, tear-filled first day scenario like we did with James. In an attempt to distract Joan from a meltdown, I opened my bag and pulled out some snacks and juice I had packed for the car ride. Sweet little Joan gobbled up every snack I handed to her within seconds. She couldn't eat fast enough. Once she had eaten every bit of food I had, she laid her head against my chest and stared out the window. I couldn't help but wonder what she was thinking. This precious baby had just been taken from everyone and everything that was familiar to her and plopped into a strange car with strange people. Even at her young age, I knew she was aware of the change in her environment and I ached for her, because, in a very small way, I knew how she felt.

I, too, was in a foreign place with foreign people speaking a foreign language. I recalled stepping off the plane at Entebbe airport, just a few days earlier, and experiencing how different everything was around me. I was acquainted with how it felt to be separated from the familiar. I, too, had a taste of what it was to be at the mercy of the people helping me, to be too exhausted and helpless to do anything on my own. I knew how that felt. And I fervently prayed that God would help Joan feel safe, cherished, and loved in my arms.

As had become customary for our Ugandan road trips, Emma played worship music from the car stereo as we drove back through the gorilla forest on the road to Kabale. After the long, difficult day we just had, this music was a balm to my soul. The songs were so familiar to me. So comforting. So much more meaningful and real to me now. I sang along and gently rubbed Joan's back as I gazed out the window. Every few minutes she would pop her head up and take an inquisitive look at me. I would smile at her and continue singing. To my pure delight, Joan eventually began singing with me. She hummed and mumbled her infantile syllables. Quietly at first.

And then Joan found her voice.

Her singing became joyfully raucous. Loud, off-pitch, gibberish. And I thought I would melt from happiness. Joan had a song to sing. None of us understood a word of it, but she sang it anyways, at the top of her lungs. As if she would burst if she didn't release it. I didn't know then that her life would be marked by the song in her heart; this melody bubbling out of her was just a glimpse of what was to come.

God had given me a flash of favor with my daughter. I was bracing myself for tears, tantrums, and heartache. I was prepared for Joan to want nothing to do with either Bradley or myself. I was expecting the worst-case scenario in a paltry attempt at self-preservation.

And God turned our first day together into a worship service.

Friend, life is hard. And often when we're knee-deep in a season of turmoil and strife, it's easy to expect the worst. Because we're experiencing the worst. It's natural to assume that every hour of every day is going to be difficult. Because this is mostly true. So when God sends you a flash of favor or a moment of unabashed happiness? Revel in it. Dive into it headfirst and let it overtake you. When your rain clouds briefly part and a sliver of sunshine slices through, close your eyes, throw your head back, and absorb every ounce of light you possibly can. You're allowed to laugh through your tears. You're allowed to dance in the rain. You're allowed to find your voice and sing through the night.

Even if nobody understands your song.

chapter 16

STUBBORN *Obedience*

Confession time: I hit a bit of a snag between finishing up Chapter 15 and beginning this chapter. It wasn't writer's block… it was much deeper than that.

- Spiritual warfare.
- Oppression.
- Depression.

It started with a series of events. I bent my ear toward certain voices in my life and gave them far too much space in my head. To put it bluntly, I was reprimanded via social media for oversharing information concerning our adoption. And it nearly derailed me. I was discouraged beyond words and seriously contemplated throwing this entire book in the trash and writing about something else. Anything else. I spiraled and sank into a dark hole of doubt. I couldn't bring myself to look at my computer or even think about putting sentences together to form a paragraph. I beat myself up for weeks.

Am I oversharing? Am I giving too many details about my family and my children? Am I ruining their lives? Am I capitalizing off my kids' trauma? Will they all need counseling? Am I a horrible mother? Why am I even writing this book in the first place? I struggled. I cried. I prayed. I read my Bible. I whined to my husband. And I sought godly counsel from trusted friends, including adult adoptees.

When I finally gathered up the courage to return to my computer today, I opened my book outline and the next part of our adoption story smacked me in the face. My struggle over the past few days and weeks suddenly made sense. Of course God was allowing me to experience setbacks during this writing process. And of course they would occur before this exact chapter—the chapter entitled "Stubborn Obedience."

We've reached a pivotal moment in our adoption journey: our court date for Joan in Kabale. I thought our time in Uganda had been difficult up to this point. We weren't prepared for the gut punch we were about to receive.

JUDGE CURMUDGEON

We awoke to a rainy, gloomy morning. We had made arrangements for Annette (Joan's social worker), Ezra (the orphanage administrator), and Peter (Joan's grandfather) to stay at the White Horse Inn the night before our court date so they could attend the hearing with us. At breakfast, George filled us in on what to expect. Our judge was a known curmudgeon—the opposite of warm and friendly. But our file was perfectly prepared. We had all the required forms and documents, as well as a blood relative willing (eager!) to sign off on our adoption. Bradley and I should only speak when spoken to. George would handle all the talking. If all went smoothly, we would be granted legal guardianship of Joan by the afternoon.

I was hopeful as our entire party crammed into Emma's SUV. We arrived at the courthouse for our 8:00 AM hearing, dressed in our best attire. James stayed in the car with Emma as the rest of us filed into the building. We were shown to a bench in the courtroom where we waited for the judge to see us. And we waited. And waited. *For two hours.* At 10:00 AM we were finally summoned into the judge's chambers; it was a small office sparsely furnished with a desk and a few chairs. Bradley and I sat next to each other with Joan sitting happily in my lap. George sat next to us, with Peter on his opposite side. Ezra and Annette stood nearby.

The judge did not look up from his notes as we entered. We sat in silence for a few minutes while he read over the paperwork in front of him. Eventually, he looked up and addressed Peter, and Peter only. They began having a conversation in their native language, which we did not understand. (By now, we were very accustomed to this recurrence.) The judge would ask a question, and Peter would answer. At one point, Peter went on a tangent, delivering a passionate monologue, hands flying, brows furrowed. I saw George's eyes grow wide and he whipped his head around, staring at Peter in horror. Both Annette's and Ezra's jaws dropped to the floor. George began to interject, but the judge put his hand up to silence him. And Peter continued.

Once George was given the opportunity to speak, words flowed quickly and he kept pointing to the stack of papers in front of the judge. Annette would chime in here and there. Ezra stood nodding in the corner. And Bradley and I sat there, utterly helpless, knowing instinctively that crap had hit the fan.

Once it appeared everybody had spoken their peace, the

judge said in English, "Let's set a date for the ruling on this case," and he pulled out his calendar and began flipping pages. And he just kept flipping those flippin' pages. Until he landed on September 25. *Three weeks away.*

This was a sucker punch to my gut. The wind was knocked out of me. It was all I could do not to fly into a hysterical fit right then and there in the judge's chamber. We wouldn't have a ruling for three eternal weeks. We were hoping to leave the courtroom with a ruling *that day.* We were expecting to be back in Dallas with our babies in three weeks. We weren't prepared for the process to drag out this long. None of this was part of our plan.

I was completely defeated as I stood up and carried Joan out of that courthouse. I was hurt all the more because the judge hadn't even looked at Bradley or me the entire time we were in his office. He never addressed us. Never greeted us or questioned us. He never gave us the opportunity to plead our case, to explain ourselves. It was as if we didn't exist to him. All he cared about was Peter.

When we loaded the car, I asked George to explain the conversation between the judge and Peter. He shook his head and told us that when asked if he consented to this adoption, Peter told the judge he had no idea who we were and he "guessed" we were taking his granddaughter to America to worship Satan. I initially laughed at the ridiculousness of this statement. But my laughter turned to anger real quick. "Why would he say that, George?! He knows exactly who we are and what we're doing! He asked us to adopt all of his grandchildren in Rutaka just two days ago!" To which George quietly replied, "I know."

WHAT AM I SUPPOSED TO DO?

When we arrived back at the hotel, George and Emma followed us to our room. Our two sweet babies sat together in the corner and played with the few toys we had with us. They were oblivious to the despair brought on by the events of the day. A cloud of sorrow settled around us. The starkness of our situation became clear. Bradley and I sat on the edge of our bed, trying to make sense of our plight.

"What are we supposed to do?" was my despondent question. George answered me directly. "Go back to Texas. We are not guaranteed a favorable ruling from the judge in Joan's case. And we do not yet have a court date secured for James. We don't know how long this will take. Joan can stay at the orphanage until your court ruling, and Emma can care for James until you return. You should go back to Texas."

Go back to Texas? *Go back to Texas? Without my children?*

The tears began to flow. George's advice sounded an awful lot like words of defeat. And throwing in the towel. Or giving up. How could we go back to Texas when God had so clearly told us to go to Uganda and bring home two babies? Making multiple trips to Uganda was never even remotely on my radar. Yet the men who were helping us and facilitating our adoption were telling us this was the best option.

Emma and George left our room, giving Bradley and me space to discuss our decision. We sat on the edge of our bed in silence for several minutes, watching our babies play sweetly in the corner. Even though we'd only had these babies with us for a few days, we had formed an incredible bond. I was madly in love. I looked at James, who had come out of his sad shell and taken an immediate interest in Joan, sharing his toys and his snacks, taking on the persona and the pride of a big brother. I looked at Joan, inexplicably happy and joyful despite her ears and stomach being infected, reveling in the attention and affection of those around her. I looked at Bradley, my dear husband, who, with tears in his eyes, was obviously experiencing the same inner turmoil that I was. "What are we supposed to do?" was my despondent question to my despondent husband.

What were we supposed to do? I'll tell you what we did.

We went back to the place of our calling. We went back to the assignment God had given to us. We went back to the clarity with which He spoke His plan for us. We went back to the multiple confirmations we had received. We went back to His Word. We dug our heels into the promises He had given us through Scripture:

> And though the Lord give you the bread of adversity and the water of affliction, yet your Teacher will not hide himself anymore, but your eyes shall see your Teacher. And your ears shall hear a word behind you, saying, 'This is the way, walk in it,' when you turn to the right or when you turn to the left. (Isaiah 30:20-21 ESV)

> Be strong and courageous; don't be terrified or afraid of them. For the Lord your God is the one who will go with you; he will not leave you or abandon you. (Deuteronomy 31:6)

> For every one of God's promises is "Yes" in him.
> Therefore, through him we also say 'Amen' to
> the glory of God. (2 Corinthians 1:20)

> He who calls you is faithful; he will surely do it.
> (1 Thessalonians 5:24 ESV)

Without question, God had called us to bring two children home from Uganda. He had opened doors, connected us with the right people, clearly revealed His plan, and confirmed our assignment over and over again. His word to us was unmistakable.

My question that day had been, *God, what are we supposed to do?* And in my moment of despair, as I began recounting God's faithfulness towards us, I heard Him ask me, *Holly, what are you supposed to do?*

And I knew what we were supposed to do.

We were supposed to stay in Uganda. We were supposed to believe God. We were supposed to trust He would finish what He started, no matter how desperate our circumstances may have appeared. It was time to focus on the voice of the Lord. It was time for big faith in a big God. It was time to draw our line in the stand. It was time to burn the ships that sailed for home. It was time for stubborn obedience.

I would stay in Uganda until every avenue had been explored and every option had been exhausted. I would stay in Uganda until the job was done. God called me to be there. I would obey Him. At any cost. My mind was made up.

WHAT I'M SUPPOSED TO DO

So here I am, writing a chapter called "Stubborn Obedience"

in a book entitled *Stubborn Obedience* that almost didn't see the light of day due to my momentary lack of stubbornness. It's no coincidence I experienced doubt and discouragement at this exact stage of writing this book. It all makes sense to me now.

This roadblock was intentional. I believe God wanted me to feel it all again. I had people telling me to quit. These voices caused me to question everything and nearly derailed me from completing the task at hand. They were the equivalent of our lawyer telling us to turn around and go back to Texas. They took the wind out of my sails and knocked the breath out of my lungs. And I found myself once again asking, *God, what am I supposed to do?* And God, in His tenderness, patience, and kindness, gently asked me in return, *Holly, what are you supposed to do?*

I know what I'm supposed to do.

I'm supposed to finish writing this book. I went back to the place of my calling. I went back to the assignment God had given me to tell of His faithfulness to our family. I remembered the clarity with which He spoke to me. I recalled the multiple confirmations He'd given me. I recognized the way He miraculously connected me with the right people on this writing journey. And today I choose to believe God. I choose to focus on the voice of the Lord. I choose to write the full account of the signs and wonders He performed on our behalf. I choose to follow Him. Even when people don't understand or they disagree with my choice. May my life boldly echo Peter's creed: "We must obey God rather than people."[i] God's relentless faithfulness to my family demands my stubborn obedience.

i Acts 5:29

chapter 17

THE WAITING WASN'T *Wasted*

We found ourselves in Uganda with time to kill. *Lots of time.* For the first two weeks we were there, it felt like we lived in Emma's SUV moving at a breakneck speed. We met James in the hospital and helped him recover from his malaria flare-up. I preached my first sermon at Emma's church. We made the journey to James' village of Muzetati to meet Agatha and Issah and acquire necessary documents. We drove over 12 hours through a gorilla forest to meet Joan at the orphanage in Kisoro, then up the mountain to Rutaka to locate Peter and gather paperwork.

We spent a gut-wrenching morning at court in Kabale, where we decided to stay in Uganda and see this thing through to the finish line, no matter what. We had a date set for a ruling in Joan's case on September 25th. We were waiting to hear back from Kampala family court as to a date for James' hearing. We gathered and submitted all paperwork. At this point, we had done all we could. And it was time to wait.

It was a bizarre reality to be in the middle of a foreign country, on this huge assignment from the Lord, and find ourselves with literally nothing to do. The "doer" in me needed a task to complete every day we were there. I needed something to accomplish. A box to check that would put us closer to our goal of obtaining guardianship of these babies and getting on the next flight back to my daughters in Texas. I'm not built to sit around and twiddle my thumbs. Patience is not my spiritual gift. When the psalmist says, *"Be still and know that I am God,"*[i] I'm pretty sure it doesn't apply to me.

Except it totally applies to me.

Because the next part of that verse says, "I will be exalted among the nations." As in, there's literally nowhere I can go that God is not sovereign and in control. Including Uganda. I had to face this truth head-on. I had to make peace with the fact that God is all-knowing and all-powerful and was working behind the scenes on my behalf, even as I waited. I had to learn how to be still and know that He is God. I had to learn that sometimes it takes more faith to do nothing than to do something.

STRENGTH WILL RISE

Isaiah 40:31 tells us, *"... those who wait for the Lord shall renew their strength."* Let's camp out here for a minute. According to this verse, strength is being renewed while we wait on the Lord. But *whose* strength is being renewed? Not God's. He has all strength. He has all power. It never depletes, so it never needs to be replenished. Isaiah 40:28 says, *"He never becomes faint or weary."* He never gets tired. He never takes a nap. (Can you imagine?) So, if *God's* strength doesn't require

---

i   Psalm 46:10

renewal, it must be *our* strength that craves rejuvenation. And this regeneration of strength happens while we wait on the Lord. It is for *our* benefit that we wait, not God's. He can do anything He wants, at any time, for anybody, without breaking a sweat. Nothing is too difficult for Him.

If God has you in a season of waiting, it's not because He's frantically scrambling behind your back, trying to figure out what to do next. He knows the end from the beginning. This season of waiting is for *your* benefit—to renew your strength, to build your faith, to expand your trust, to stretch your patience, to draw you closer to Him. Your waiting is never wasted, Friend. It holds divine purpose. But you must first be willing to be still and know that He is God.

Being still doesn't necessarily mean sitting around, twiddling your thumbs, and basking in boredom. Thank God. Being still refers to the posture of our hearts and minds. It means our striving comes to a halt, and we relinquish the outcome to God's capable hands. It means we can exhale, knowing God's got the details covered. It means we're free to dance through our difficulties. It means we can laugh through adversity. It means we can rest, even in the middle of our trials. We are still when we realize that God is God and we are not. We are still when we acknowledge He is in complete control. We are still when we are free.

WHILE WE WAITED

Bradley and I decided to be still and stay busy. We figured

we'd serve the Lord while we were waiting on Him. We also made up our minds to soak in every ounce of Ugandan culture as we possibly could with the extra time on our hands.

The Saturday after we returned to Kampala from Kabale was an extraordinary day. Emma's church, Passion Christian Assembly, was growing in number every week. People came from all over the city to hear the gospel preached clearly. Dozens were coming to faith in Christ, and they were ready for water baptism. Because the church didn't yet have its own building, we loaded up the entire congregation on buses and took a day trip to Lake Victoria. We held an outdoor church service on the shore. Bradley preached, holding Joan in his arms, and I led worship, with James at my feet. Bystanders heard the gospel message and several received Jesus as their Lord and Savior on the spot. When it was time for baptism, Bradley handed Joan to me, took off his shoes, and waded out into the ice-cold water of the lake. As an ordained pastor, he had the honor of baptizing the new believers in Lake Victoria that day. What a privilege it was to serve the Lord while we waited.

The very next day was Sunday. Since Passion Christian Assembly had their service the day before on the lake, Emma had a "day off" and took us to worship at Watoto Church, an affiliate of Hillsong Church. Their service felt so familiar. They had a killer band, praise team, and a full choir in the loft. They sang songs we knew. There was great lighting, a fancy sound system, and screens with words. Yet it still felt very Ugandan. Their children's choir sang and danced in the aisles, people worshiped with streamers and tambourines, and we almost died from heatstroke because there was no air conditioning.

That church service felt like home—but better. Because I was the minority. There weren't very many people in that sanctuary who looked like me and I loved it. It was a great reminder of the diversity of the Kingdom of God. Every tribe, tongue, and nation will be represented in heaven, worshiping the same God, in whose colorful image we were all created. That Sunday morning service at Watoto Church was a gift. What a joy it was to worship the Lord while we waited.

We spent the first part of the following week resting at our hotel, visiting the mall playground, and helping Emma at Care Medical Center, the pro-life ministry he founded—where there is never a dull moment. We prayed for the pregnant mothers who were there to deliver, we snuggled newborn babies, we served food to sick patients, and we played with children in the street. Everywhere we looked, there was somebody who needed encouragement, or prayer, or a smile. What a blessing it was to care for God's people while we waited.

Towards the end of the week, we took a day trip out to the city of Jinja, about two hours east of Kampala. Emma's SUV was (of course) packed. His beautiful wife Sarah joined us, as well as his darling daughter Catrina (who was Joan's age), and sweet little Job (who my best friend Dianna was in the process of adopting). You add in Bradley, James, Joan, and me, and the babies officially outnumbered the adults. Jinja was beautiful, nestled against the northern banks of Lake Victoria. The landscape was lush, the shops were quaint, the people were friendly. Bradley and I took the babies on a river cruise, where we visited the source of the Nile River. It flows north all the way through South Sudan, Sudan, and Egypt, eventually emptying out into the Mediterranean Sea. (This will never not blow my mind.) We ended our day in Jinja at the house of Emma's mother, JaJa (grandmother) Margaret. JaJa prepared a feast of goat, rice, beans, matooke, and cassava. Several of the neighborhood children heard of JaJa's "Mzungu" visitors and came around to catch a glimpse of us. We ate and laughed until darkness fell and it was time to return to Kampala. What a thrill it was to fellowship with other believers while we waited.

The following Sunday, Bradley and I were guests at Cross Healing Ministries Church in Kampala—almost the exact opposite situation from Watoto Church. Cross Healing was held in an open-air building with a dirt floor and folding chairs. No fancy lights, no words on screens, no slick band. Instead of a choir, they had a praise dance team. These people had the Holy Ghost in their hips and expressed their praise through movement. I've never felt more white in my entire life. Bradley and I were invited onstage to minister through song. And God showed up that day. His presence doesn't require technology, or smoke machines, or contemporary music. His presence rests on those who worship Him in spirit and in truth, even if it's on a dirt floor. What a gift it was to dwell in His presence while we waited.

The next morning, we received incredible news from our lawyer, George: we had a court date scheduled for James' hearing on September 20th! This report brought such encouragement, because it meant we could possibly have this thing wrapped up and be home by the first of October! For the first time in quite a while, I felt hopeful. I felt like we were still on the right track. I felt like our process was finally moving forward. What a relief it was to know that God was working on our behalf while we waited.

That same day, we had a timely visitor all the way from Dallas. A gentleman by the name of Charlie Loper made his annual trip to Uganda to work with his ministry, Master Cares. He brought with him a double stroller to help me maneuver around town easier with two babies. I could not fathom a more necessary gift! What a wonder it was to know God was providing for us while we waited.

Those long days of waiting in Uganda turned out to be amazingly fruitful because Bradley and I made the decision to serve the Lord while we waited on Him to come through for us. Instead of sitting around our hotel room, whining about how things weren't going our way, wringing our hands with worry, we put our hands to work and became occupied with ministry. We found out that you can "be still" and be effective at the same time. Instead of killing time, we planted seeds; seeds of service, love, faith, trust, worship, and prayer. These seeds will always produce a bountiful harvest of blessing. These seeds will prove that God has a good future planned for those He loves. These seeds will cause strength to rise while we wait on the Lord.

Those days of waiting were for our benefit. It was good for us to wait because lives were impacted by our service. It was good for us to wait because we entered into a deeper season of worship. It was good for us to wait because we met new people and experienced new places. It was good for us to wait because we saw the provision of the Lord with our own eyes. It was good for us to wait because our strength was renewed. It was good for us to wait because we were given more time to bond with our new babies. It was all for our benefit.

While our hearts and minds were still, our hands were working for the Lord.

And our waiting wasn't wasted.

chapter 18

I PUT MY HEART
on a Plane

September 20th rolled around, and we braced ourselves for James's hearing at Family Court in downtown Kampala. As with Joan's court date, we had all our documents and paperwork perfectly prepared and ready to be presented. We had sworn affidavits from Agatha and Issah verifying James was indeed an orphan with no known parents. We had police records from Muzetati, validating the search efforts for his family. We had all necessary certificates and forms. This case was very black and white. No question marks or holes in the story. George was hopeful we would get a swift ruling from the judge in Kampala.

We sat in the crowded waiting room at the downtown courthouse for several hours, waiting for the clerk to call our names. We brought snacks and juice for James and Joan, as well as toys to keep them occupied. Nobody seemed to be in a rush. One by one, I watched as other names got called ahead of us to go see the judge. Remember in the last chapter when I said patience is not my spiritual gift? God found multiple ways of building my patience during this adoption process. And one of them was sitting in a Ugandan courthouse waiting room. With two babies. For three hours. Thank you, God.

Our names were finally called. We followed George back to the judge's chambers where we sat in an office warmly furnished, decorated with pictures of who I could only assume was the judge's family. I immediately felt at ease. This judge seemed to be a family man. Surely he would be friendlier and nicer than the judge we saw in Joan's case.

And he *was* friendlier and nicer than the previous judge. Not only did he acknowledge our presence, but he spoke directly to us, asking questions about our family life back in Texas. He took an interest in our story. He cared about what we were doing. But he also wasn't satisfied with our perfectly prepared paperwork. The affidavits provided by Issah, Agatha, and the Muzetati police were not enough to convince him James wasn't kidnapped from Kenya. He wanted to personally speak with all parties involved. Furthermore, he wanted to see James' medical records. He looked me directly in the eye and said, "These kids come with all kinds of diseases. I want you to know exactly what you're getting." I believe he meant it kindly, but this statement appalled me. He spoke of James as if he wasn't an actual human being. As if some illness or sickness would deter me from following through with this adoption. As if a disease would nullify the process. And nothing could have been farther from the truth. This child was worthy of love and acceptance and a family, regardless of his medical history, which we were now required to submit to the court.

We made plans to come back with Issah, Agatha, and the chief of police from Muzetati, so the judge could question everyone involved. He looked at Bradley next and said, "We won't require both parents at the next hearing." I looked at my husband, knowing exactly what this statement meant. The judge scheduled our next court date for October 2nd, and my hopes of being back in Texas by the first of October went out the window. Bradley and I each grabbed a baby in one arm and held each other's hand as we exited the judge's office. With tears flowing down my cheeks, I clung to my husband for dear life, because I knew.

It was time for Bradley to go home to Texas.

At this point, we had been in Uganda for three weeks. We had been away from our daughters for three weeks. And we desperately missed them. As much as it killed me to think about being in Uganda by myself with two babies, it made me deliriously happy to know that my daughters in Texas would have a parent there with them. Bradley had done everything required of him in Uganda. His presence was no longer necessary for our next court date, any meetings at the immigration office, or the U.S. Embassy. I could accomplish everything else by myself. It was time for Bradley to go home.

We purchased a plane ticket for the very next day.

A PRAYING HUSBAND

I'm not sure I have the vocabulary to accurately sum up how I felt watching Bradley pack up his suitcase that night, preparing for his journey home while I lay in the middle of our hotel bed with my eyes glazed over. James and Joan sat on the floor in our kitchenette, playing with their toys, oblivious to my pain. The weight of everything was piling up. It would be yet another two weeks until our second court hearing for James and we still were not certain if we would get a favorable ruling from Joan's judge. Meanwhile, the love of my life was packing up to leave me by myself in a foreign country where I would be responsible for caring for two babies by myself, not knowing if/when this process would be complete and I would be able to fly home. The heaviness of it all was unbearable.

That night, after we put the babies to bed, Bradley prayed over me. Having a husband who storms heaven on my behalf is one of the greatest comforts of my life. He prayed that God would be with me and strengthen me in the coming weeks. He prayed that God would give me the endurance needed to complete the assignment. He prayed that God would finish what He started. As Bradley prayed, I sobbed.

"What if our girls have forgotten who I am?" I cried. "Will you talk to them about me? Will you tell them how desperately I miss them? Will you let them know I think about them every minute of every day? Will you tell them mommy loves them?"

Bradley assured me that he would. In my moment of heartache, my husband wrapped his arms around me. As he held me, he gave me the most amazing compliment that will stay with me until I die. "Our girls will never forget who their mother is. They have the very best in you. You are the crown of our family." And I knew this for certain: if Bradley Knight was the head of our household, then I was honored to be his crown. I have a good man.

The next morning was a blur. I knew Bradley would be leaving me, and my coping mechanism was to ignore my emotions and pretend everything was okay. I didn't want my final few hours with my husband spent teary-eyed and snot-nosed. We spent the nearly hour-long drive to Entebbe airport in silence, clutching hands with white knuckles, each with a baby in our lap in the back seat of Emma's SUV. The waterworks began once we pulled up to the passenger drop-off area. I got out of the car and wept on Bradley's shoulder. I could hear him crying, too. He let go of me and kissed our babies goodbye. And I watched my heart walk into the airport to board a plane that would take him to the other side of the globe. Back to our home. Back to our daughters. Back to our life.

Emma drove me and my babies back to our hotel. I put James and Joan down for their naps, then dropped to my knees in our kitchenette. This was it. The loneliest I'd ever felt in my life. Isolated and alone on a cold linoleum floor in the middle of Uganda.

PEACE THAT PASSES UNDERSTANDING

God had removed every crutch I was prone to lean on. I was in a foreign land with foreign people. I was adjusting to new foods, new scents, new scenery every day. I was caring for two babies who, in many ways, were still strangers to me. I was unable to move about freely and drive myself places. I was at the mercy of other people's kindness. I was thousands of miles away from my support system: my family, my friends, my church. I was separated from my three daughters, who were the objects of my purpose and identity. And now my rock, my stability, my foundation, my glue, my security, *my husband*, was removed from me. Every comfort, every convenience, every companion was gone.

And yet.

I had peace.

I'm not saying this to sound trite or super-spiritual. You've been with me on this journey long enough now to know I'm neither of those things. I don't want to sugarcoat this in any way. Yes, I was in deep pain. Yes, I was in agony. Yes, I was suffering. Yet, at the same time, I was at peace. I can't explain it. Which makes sense because the peace God gives is beyond our understanding.[i]

I had peace on that lonely day in Uganda because peace is a by-product of obedience. Isaiah 32:17 says, "The result of righteousness will be peace; the effect of righteousness will be quiet confidence forever." What is righteousness? It's right standing with God. How do we gain this right standing with God? By putting our faith in Jesus Christ and accepting the redemption available to us through His death, burial, and resurrection. How do we live righteously? By communing with Jesus, walking in accordance with His Word (the Bible), and obeying His commands. Stubbornly. Even if it means you end up alone on a linoleum floor in a foreign country. The result of this righteousness is peace. The effect of this surrender is quiet confidence. The product of this obedience is inner tranquility—100 percent of the time.

Unexplainable peace is an indicator you're on the right track. Your situation may be bleak. Your life may have been flipped upside down. Your world may have seemingly come to an end. *And yet.* You can have peace. You can have quiet confidence. This divine peace is one of the sweetest fruits of

---

i   Philippians 4:7

being smack-dab in the middle of God's will, because you can experience it regardless of the upheaval happening around you. God's peace is not circumstantial, it's consequential. Meaning, it's the result of walking with the Lord. It's fruit produced by the indwelling Holy Spirit of God in our lives.[ii] Jesus tells us in John 14:27, "Peace I leave with you. My peace I give to you. I do not give to you as the world gives. Don't let your heart be troubled or fearful." Following Jesus yields peace. When the world tells you to be fearful, you can be peaceful. When you face heartache and trouble, your heart and mind will be guarded by peace that surpasses understanding.[iii] This is God's promise to us.

Do you need peace today, Friend? Good grief, I know I do. Even if you're not personally going through a trial, all you have to do is turn on the news for 60 seconds to know this world is crazy. Right has become wrong. Up is now down. Evil masquerades as good. In these days of violence, division, pandemic, political unrest, war, and natural disasters, God's people should be marked by peace. We should remain above the fray. We should be identified by our steadfastness and tranquility. And here's the beautiful part: we don't have to strive for this peace. We don't have to work for it. And we definitely can't manufacture it. It's our inheritance. It's our birthright as daughters of the king. It's our identity as followers of Christ. Peace is our reality when we walk in obedience. "Blessed are the peacemakers."[iv] That's us, sweet Friend.

Complete surrender to Jesus will most likely take you to the

---

ii   Galatians 5:22
iii   Philippians 4:7
iv   Matthew 5:9

end of yourself. At some point, you may find yourself stripped of every comfort, convenience, and companion. Your crutches will be taken away. And when you're left standing alone—if your feet are planted on the promises of God—you will be saturated in peace. I was literally left standing alone in a foreign country, with a seemingly endless road still ahead of me. The light at the end of my tunnel was not yet visible. I had nobody around me to turn to or lean on. *And yet.* I had peace. Beyond my comprehension. I found it on my knees on a cold linoleum floor in the middle of Uganda. And it was the direct result of my stubborn obedience.

chapter 19

Blindsided

God has never been blindsided. Isn't that a comforting truth? He's never been surprised or shocked by a turn of events. He's never said, "I didn't see that coming!" He's never scratched His head and wondered what to do next. He's never been caught unaware. He's never been confused or bewildered in any situation at any time.

I cannot say the same for myself.

I have definitely been blindsided by life. I imagine you have been, too. I've been knocked in the jaw by events I didn't see coming. I have panicked and wondered what to do next. I have been confused, shocked, and bewildered by situations. I have asked why God would allow certain things to happen. I have questioned His goodness. My faith has been shaken.

Two days after putting Bradley on a plane back to Texas, I was blindsided to such an extent it's painful for me to relive it and write about it, even now—nine years later. It was the lowest day of my life. And I hit rock bottom.

It was Sunday. James, Joan, and I were picked up from our hotel and driven to Passion Christian Assembly, where we worshiped with fellow believers who were now our friends.

James and Joan were familiar with the other children and quickly left my side to play with their little mates. I sat on a row with Emma's wife, Sarah, and his sisters, Hadija and Cathy. We sang simple, familiar songs, filling the open-air building with our exuberant praises. Emma preached a soul-nourishing message, then invited me and my babies to his house for an equally soul-nourishing meal.

Emma's house was a nonstop party. His doors were always open to those in need. At that time, he and Sarah had living with them around seven school-aged children whose parents couldn't care for them for various reasons. His sisters and his nephew also lived with him. Much like his SUV, his house stayed packed.

While we were waiting for lunch to be prepared, the children practiced songs for an upcoming church performance. Their clear voices sang out familiar lyrics: "Cast your burdens unto Jesus because he cares for you. Higher, higher, lift up Jesus higher. Lower, lower, lower Satan lower." I, too, had sung this song as a child. I sat on Emma's couch soaking up the concert of a lifetime with these kids.

Lunch was served. Out of necessity, I had become a very adventurous eater in Uganda. The creature comforts of Chick-Fil-A and Tex-Mex fajitas weren't readily available, so I had to eat what was served to me and be grateful for it. Today's culinary adventure? A whole fried tilapia from Lake Victoria, *with its eyes still attached.* Emma sat the plate in front of me. "What am I supposed to do with the eyes?" I gasped. "Eat them. They're delicious" was his unwelcomed response. To my horror, he reached down to the plate, plucked the eyes out of the tilapia's head, and popped them in his mouth with a satisfied look on his face. He then went on to instruct me as to how to put bites of fish in my mouth, remove the bones with my teeth, then take the fish out of my mouth and *feed it to my children*. I had a million questions, but my kids were hungry so I did as I was told. Despite the unconventional consumption methods, the meal was delicious. James, Joan, and I ate our fill.

We returned to the hotel for naptime. Sunday afternoon naps are something like a religion in the Knight house, and these babies needed to be baptized into this religion as early as possible. While in Uganda, I spent most naptimes reading my Bible, catching up on emails, checking social media, and updating my blog. I craved these quiet moments every afternoon. I needed this time to myself just as much as my growing babies needed their rest.

During this particular naptime, I listened to music in our hotel room's kitchenette. Our church choir back in Texas was in the process of recording a new album, and Bradley was sending me mixes of the finished songs as they came in from the audio engineer. I worshiped along as I listened to songs like "Standing on His Promises," "I Choose to Worship," and "I'll Trust You." It was my second worship service of the day, but this time the only people in attendance were me and the Lord. He met me in the kitchenette as I praised Him that afternoon.

When the kids woke up from their nap, we went outside to our hotel's courtyard to play and stretch our legs. We had acquired a few bouncy balls that James enjoyed kicking around and chasing. Joan was still wobbly on her feet, but she trailed after him to the best of her ability. The weather was beautiful and the golden-hour sky was radiant.

We ate dinner out on the patio of our hotel's restaurant. After my adventurous lunch, I ordered a safe spaghetti Bolognese and chicken tenders for the kids to share. James and Joan bounced along to the background music softly playing around us, the calypso beat in their bones. We watched the sun set and the stars began to sparkle.

After dinner, I took the babies upstairs for bath time. I use the phrase "bath" very loosely because we didn't have a bathtub in our hotel. Instead, I had a large plastic bucket I filled with warm water every night and bathed one child at a time. The kids loved splashing in their bucket and watching the water spill over the edges. I let them each linger there for as long as they were happy. It was during this nightly ritual I learned the importance of properly moisturizing their beautiful skin. Regular lotion wouldn't cut it. They required a thick cream or oil to fully hydrate their dry skin. Once it absorbed, I dressed them in comfy pajamas for bed. There is nothing more delicious than a freshly bathed and lotioned Ugandan baby. They were edible. I drank in their scent as we snuggled, wishing them to stay little forever. Joan, in particular, would eagerly let me embrace her. She craved the attention and welcomed my hugs. And I gladly gave them.

Before tucking them into bed, we sang a few songs ("Baby Jesus" was their favorite), read three books, and said our prayers. James and Joan were both wildly active during the day and fell asleep hard and fast every night. I kissed both of them over and over again, turned off their bedroom light, and closed the door. I could hear them talking and giggling for a few minutes before the room went radio silent. They were asleep.

Downton Abbey was my escape every evening. Once

I knew the kids were conked out, I'd fix myself a cup of tea, wrap a blanket around me, and prop my iPad on the table in our kitchenette. Sometimes I would stress eat a bowl of cheap ramen noodles or order another bowl of spaghetti Bolognese to be delivered to the room. This is how I made it through. The Dowager Countess of Grantham took my mind off my bleak reality every night.

And so I sat at our table, wrapped in a blanket, consumed with Lady Mary Crawley's love life when I was blindsided by an unexpected knock on my hotel door.

It was Emma and his sister Cathy. They had come to take Joan.

It took me a few minutes to comprehend what they meant by "take Joan."

"Take her where?!" I frantically asked.

They were taking her back to Kabale for the judge's ruling in two days, September 25th. She had to be present for the ruling. Emma and Cathy would take her by bus and carry her to court.

"When will you bring her back to me?!" I needed to know.

They would bring her back to me in three days, if we received a favorable ruling.

"What if we're not granted custody?!" Dear God, I hadn't let my mind go there, yet. The tears started flowing.

The answer was swift and sharp. If we were not awarded guardianship of Joan, she would immediately be taken back to the orphanage in Kisoro. And I would never see her again.

"You can't take her tonight! She's asleep! Come back and get her tomorrow!" I was grasping at straws.

I was instructed to pack a bag of Joan's belongings, diapers, sippy cups, snacks, clothes, and toys. Emma and Cathy would need all these supplies for their 12-hour bus ride, which left Kampala at 5:00am the following morning.

"I didn't know you were coming tonight! Why didn't you tell me you were coming to get her? Why didn't you warn me? Emma, you can't take her from me!"

But even as I stood there screaming through tears, my dear friend opened the bedroom door and stepped inside to get Joan. She awoke, cheerful as ever, happy to see her friends Emma and Cathy. She smiled and reached for me when she saw me. I snatched her up and held onto her like my life depended on it. Because it did.

As I clung to her, my mind kept telling me this could be the last time I ever held this baby. But my heart refused to accept this possibility. The facts were that we may not receive custody of Joan on September 25th, but my faith said I had been sent to Uganda by God to adopt this baby girl and she was meant to be mine. My heart shattered as my mind quickly locked onto the worst-case scenario. My head was spinning. I was sobbing. Everything was happening so quickly; I was unable to process it all.

"We must take her now." Emma interrupted my thoughts.

I let her go. Emma was a trusted friend who, in a very short period of time, had become my brother. He loved me and I loved him. He knew taking Joan from me would cause me great pain. He knew we may not get the outcome we hoped for. He knew the risks involved. He knew the grief I was experiencing. But he also knew the plan. He knew the due process. And he would do the right thing, even when it hurt. Emma was a trustworthy friend.

So I let him take Joan.

He and Cathy walked out of my hotel room, carrying my darling, happy, freshly bathed baby, along with all her belongings. I had no assurance of ever seeing her again.

This was my rock bottom.

I told you at the beginning of this chapter I have a hard time letting my mind go back to this night. I hate reliving this moment. I am literally experiencing a mild anxiety episode even as I sit here and type. My breathing is labored and I can't catch my breath. I'm overheated and my skin is red and splotchy. The depth of despair I felt that lonely Sunday night in Uganda is something I'll never forget for as long as I live.

It was the lowest point of my entire life.

I sat there in my hotel kitchenette, drowning in pain, feeling completely and utterly alone, facing the possibility of never seeing my daughter again, with my son sound asleep in his bed. All my hopes, all my dreams, all the months of planning and preparation, all the work we'd already done, all the love I felt for this baby girl... all of it walked out the door with Emma that night. I was desperately hopeless. I had nobody to turn to. Nobody to comfort me. Nobody to cry with. Nobody to care for me.

What would you have done if you were in my position? If you had just been blindsided to such an extent? Maybe you're reading this book and you don't have to imagine being in a position like mine. Maybe you're well-acquainted with what it feels like to lose a child. Or maybe you've been blindsided by a cancer diagnosis, or yet another miscarriage, or an unfaithful spouse. The fact of the matter is, being blindsided by bad news accompanies every human being walking on this earthly sod. It doesn't make it any easier, but pain comes with the territory. It's part of life. And it sucks.

So what did I do when I was blindsided on that lonely Sunday night in Uganda?

I worshiped.

I had already experienced two worship services earlier that day. It was now time for my third and most important. I walked over to my computer and opened the email containing the new songs Bradley had sent me earlier that day. I clicked on the song, "I'll Trust You." I knelt down on that cold linoleum floor, placed both hands top on my head, and sang over myself:

> You are my refuge, in you I'll trust.
> You are my fortress, in you I'll trust.
> I won't dread the terror by night,
> For angels are all around me.
> So I will not fear.
> When I call you, you'll answer in time of trouble.
> When I call you, you'll answer. You will deliver.
> Oh, I'll trust you, for I will dwell under your shadow.
> I won't dread the terror by night,
> For angels are all around me.
> So I will not fear.[10]

I repeated the phrase, "I'll trust you, I'll trust you, I'll trust you," over and over and over again. It became the air in my lungs. The blood in my veins. The strength of my heart. "I'll trust you" became my battle cry.

Because You are trustworthy, God. *I'll trust you.*

Even when I'm blindsided. *I'll trust you.*

Even when I don't know how things will turn out.
I'll trust you.

Even when I'm suffocated by pain. *I'll trust you.*

Even when I'm separated from everyone I love.
I'll trust you.

Even when I'm at rock bottom. *I'll trust you.*

Following God in stubborn obedience means walking in complete trust, even when it doesn't make sense. I was on assignment from God. Accomplishing His plan. Listening to His voice. I was completely surrendered to Him. I was at His mercy. I had no other option than to trust Him. And, as I mentioned at the beginning of this chapter, God wasn't blindsided on that Sunday night. He wasn't shocked Emma came to take Joan from me. He wasn't scratching His head. He never broke a sweat. He had a plan all along, and it was glorious. But I had to be willing to trust Him without having all the details.

Hitting rock bottom is a mysterious thing. The phrase "rock bottom" implies that you can't go any lower, that you've hit the rock at the bottom of your pit, or drank all the poison from your glass down to the rocks (ice). Your life literally cannot get any worse. However, in my experience as a follower of Christ, I've learned that when I'm at my lowest, there's always a Rock under me:

> The Lord is my rock, my strength. The Lord is my
> rock, my fortress, and my deliverer, my God, my
> rock where I seek refuge, my shield and the horn

of my salvation, my stronghold. (Psalm 18:2)

I call you to from the ends of the earth when my heart is without strength. Lead me to the rock that is higher than I, for you have been a refuge for me, a strong tower in the face of the enemy. (Psalm 61:2-3)

The Rock – his work is perfect; all his ways are just. A faithful God, without bias, he is righteous and true. (Deuteronomy 32:4)

The worship service that took place on the cold floor that night was the most significant of my life. I was at my lowest, but I encountered my Rock. I experienced what it means to be held, to be covered, to be sustained. As I surrendered my sorrow, He poured out His power. I was able to stand. I was able to continue breathing. I was able to sleep peacefully that night knowing God was in control.

Friend, I pray you believe this with every fiber of your being today. No matter how you've been blindsided by life, God is good and He is for you. He is your strength. He is your deliverer. He is your refuge. He is your comforter. He is your help. He is your salvation. He is your trustworthy friend.

And when you hit rock bottom, you're held by the Rock of Ages.

chapter 20

Akansasira

I don't recall any details about how I made it through the next day, Monday, September 24, 2012. I'm pretty sure I've blocked this day from my memory completely. I knew Emma and Cathy were on a bus to Kabale with my darling Joan, and I knew we'd receive a ruling on her case the following day. I knew I had to keep busy. I knew I had to take care of James. But I don't remember any of it. I was in a fog. I was in survival mode.

I was up early the morning of Tuesday, September 25th. My phone was blowing up with people calling and texting from Texas, asking for updates. I received countless messages on Facebook from strangers who were planning on staying up all night long, praying for a favorable ruling from the judge. My inbox was full of encouraging emails from friends and family. This could be the absolute best day of my life, or the absolute worst. The stakes were high.

I received a phone call from Emma around 10:00 AM informing me the judge had not yet arrived at court, and the ruling was being delayed for at least an hour. Of course. I knew better than to expect this day to run on schedule. I had been in

Uganda for long enough to know that things rarely happened in a timely fashion.

I pulled out my Bible in an attempt to take my mind off of my situation and focus on the Lord. I tried not to think about our horrible court date three weeks earlier, and how the judge wouldn't even make eye contact with us. I tried not to recall Peter's horrible words about us wanting to take Joan to America to worship Satan. I tried not to remember how hopeless this case felt. I tried not to be discouraged. I found myself saying out loud, *"God, you've got to come through for us. You must come through. We need you. Please, God. Help us."*

And He did.

Two very long hours later, around noon on Tuesday, September 25th, I received a second phone call from Emma. I was officially the proud mother of a little Ugandan girl. Akansasira Joan was ours. God came through. And it was the best day of my life.

I immediately dialed Bradley's number. It was 3:00 AM in Texas, but I knew he had his ringer turned on, waiting for my call. Through tears, I told him, "We have a fourth daughter. She's ours." I could hardly believe the words as I said them. He began to weep and quietly said, "Praise God." Yes. Praise God.

It would be another 36 hours until I could hold my baby girl again. Emma and Cathy wouldn't return to Kampala until the following day. But all was well with the world. I would see Joan again. I would hold her again. Kiss her again. Bathe her again. Feed her again. Hear her laugh again. Comfort her again. She was mine and I was hers. Just as God had promised.

NEW NAME

Our new daughter's birth name was Akansasira Joan, but we had long ago decided to change her name. It all began when I was pregnant with my third daughter, Harper Ryan. We had chosen her name months before she was born. Harper had a classy ring to it, and Ryan is Bradley's middle name. We had her name stitched into blankets, towels, and onesies. Her monogram was everywhere. But the night before she was born, I had a full-on freak-out panic attack. The name "Jolie Danielle" popped into my head and I just *knew* this would be my daughter's name. "Jolie" is after my dad, Joel. "Danielle" is for Bradley's dad, Danny. "Jolie Danielle" was the perfect name to honor both grandfathers.

"We have to change her name! She should be Jolie Danielle, not Harper Ryan! We've made a huge mistake!" I protested. But to no avail. Bradley and my mom ganged up on me and convinced me that our third (and final! LOL) daughter's name should be Harper Ryan. Ava and Greta had already been calling her Harper. Her monogram was everywhere. It was too late to go back. And so I mourned the loss of the beautiful name "Jolie Danielle"… until that special day when we received the email stating we had been matched with two children in Uganda. Mumwata James and Akansasira Joan.

Joan?! That's remarkably similar to Jolie. "Will I be able to change her name?" was my question to Emma. "Of course. Once she's yours," he assured me. This baby girl was my Jolie Danielle. She was supposed to have this name all along. It was always meant for her.

It was very important to Bradley and me that Jolie also had

a Ugandan name. We were proud of her heritage and prayed she would be, too. We didn't want her to lose this part of her identity. She will always be Ugandan. I mentioned in Chapter 10, the meaning of names in Uganda is very significant. Most Ugandans have a religious name and a clan name, and these names can be used interchangeably. Jolie's clan name given at birth was Akansasira. I did a little investigating and was overjoyed to discover that *Akansasira* means "God has been merciful to me," or "God has shown me mercy." What a lovely name. What a beautiful picture. What a wonderful Savior.

Not only is Jolie's life story a demonstration of the radical love of God, but her very name is a sermon, in and of itself.

JOLIE

As I mentioned before, Jolie is derived from the name "Joel," which was my late father's name. It also happens to be the name of a small book tucked into the Old Testament. Joel is considered a minor prophet. Little was known about his life, his family, or his profession, yet he was one of the first biblical authors to write about the "Day of the Lord," or coming judgment. Joel 2:1 says, "Blow the horn in Zion; sound the alarm on my holy mountain! Let all the residents of the land tremble, for the day of the Lord is coming; in fact, it is near."

At this point in time, the people of Judah had assumed God's judgment would be reserved for pagan nations, and they would escape God's wrath as His chosen people. Joel let them know that this was simply not true. God is just and His justice will be poured out on all people. Only those who have repented of their sins and turned from their wickedness would be fully restored to God. Joel 2:32 tells us: "Then everyone who calls on the name of the Lord will be saved." This was the escape route. This was the path to restoration with God. The Israelite's heritage would not spare them on the Day of the Lord. Only those who called on the name of the Lord would be saved.

The name *Joel* means "Jehovah is God." It's a picture of God's holiness, righteousness, and justice. Much like the theme of the Old Testament book, the name Joel depicts that God's judgment is inevitable. God must judge sin because He is holy. God must pour out His wrath because He is righteous. God must condemn wickedness because He is just. (This sounds like a lot of bad news. But good news is coming.)

DANIELLE

Danielle is the feminine version of the name "Daniel," which is a nod to Bradley's father, Danny. Daniel is also a book in the Old Testament, considered major prophecy. In the first half, Daniel chronicles his exile in Babylon, describing events that have become well-known to those of us who grew up in church. You may have heard about three young Jewish men who were thrown into a fiery furnace for refusing to worship King Nebuchadnezzar's golden statue. Jesus himself joined Shadrach, Meshach, and Abednego in that blazing inferno, and they were delivered without a hair on their head being singed.[i] Maybe you'll recall the story of Daniel himself being thrown into a den full of hungry lions. His crime? Consistently praying to the one

---

i   Daniel 3:8-30

true God. But God sent an angel to shut the mouths of those lions, and Daniel was released, completely unharmed.[ii]

The second half of Daniel gives prophetic insight into the rise and fall of earthly empires and the formation of God's future kingdom on earth. It details His coming judgment. In fact, much like Joel, Daniel literally means *"God is my judge."* Daniel 2:44 describes this coming judgment: "In the days of those kings, the God of the heavens will set up a kingdom that will never be destroyed, and this kingdom will not be left to another people. It will crush all these kingdoms and bring them to an end, but will itself endure forever." God's judgment is inevitable. And so is His kingdom.

AKANSASIRA

We've made it to the good news: Jolie's Ugandan name, Akansasira, "God has been merciful to me." Maybe you're reading this today and you've never been introduced to the God of all mercy. Perhaps you resonate with the previous paragraphs about God's judgment and wrath. Sometimes it's easier to picture God as vengeful and just than it is to view Him as kind and compassionate. Can we chat about His mercy for a moment? According to Merriam-Webster, *mercy* is defined as "compassion or forbearance shown especially to an offender."[11] In our case, we are the offender, and God is compassionate. Paul's theology on mercy in his letter to the Ephesians is our guide:

"...We were by nature children under wrath...

---

ii   Daniel 6:16-24

But God, who is rich in mercy, because of his great love that he had for us, made us alive with Christ even though we were dead in trespasses. You are saved by grace! He also raised us up with him and seated us with him in the heavens in Christ Jesus, so that in the coming ages he might display the immeasurable riches of his grace through his kindness to us in Christ Jesus."[iii]

Did you catch all that? Because of God's rich mercy, we who were dead in our sins (that's all of us) are now made alive! Because of God's mercy, we are saved by grace! Because of God's mercy, we have been elevated above our circumstances and are seated in heavenly places with Christ Jesus. We have a new life, a new purpose, and a new perspective. All because of God's great mercy.

Jolie's life is a beautiful picture of the mercy of God. She was sick, lost, abandoned, and alone. But God had mercy on her and gave her a new existence. Her life portrays the apostle Peter's words, "Once you were not a people, but now you are God's people; you had not received mercy, but now you have received mercy"[iv] I want to be clear and emphasize this as much as I possibly can: I am not Jolie's savior. Bradley is not Jolie's savior. *Jesus* is Jolie's savior. He had a plan for her all along. We were merely a conduit of His plan to give her a new life and a new purpose. Jolie is now counted as "God's people" and is seated in heavenly places with Jesus Christ, because she has

---

iii   Ephesians 2:3-7
iv   1 Peter 2:10

been introduced to the God of all mercy.

HER FULL NAME

Jolie Danielle Akansasira. This name combines layers of deep meaning. "Jolie" for her late maternal grandfather, Joel: a faithful minister of the gospel until his death, a kind leader, a consistent worshiper, a loyal friend. "Danielle" after her paternal grandfather, Danny: also a faithful minister of the gospel, a wise shepherd, a steady companion, a trustworthy ally. Jolie now has a rich heritage of faith on both sides of her family. She has been grafted into a lineage of Christ-followers and her inheritance is robust, filled with generational blessings to which she now has access. This is the glory of adoption.

But her name also holds glory for you and me. The biblical meaning of her combined name is *"Jehovah God, my Judge, had mercy on me."* Friend, don't let this truth slip past you today. Jehovah God, Yahweh, the great I AM, the One who was and is and is to come, the God of judgment, wrath, and righteousness—*this God loves you* and chose to pour His mercy out on *you*. He is the God of all mercy. And in case you feel as if you don't deserve His mercy, please be assured that it never runs out. It's new every morning. There's literally nothing you can do to exhaust God's mercy. You are the object of His affection. You are His pride and joy. Through the death, burial, and resurrection of Jesus Christ, you have been adopted into the family of God. Peter said it best:

> Because of his great mercy he has given us new
> birth and a living hope through the resurrection of

Jesus Christ from the dead and into an inheritance that is imperishable, undefiled, and unfading, kept in heaven for you.[v]

You are no longer who you once were. You are a new creation with a new name. You now have access to a glorious inheritance. You now have the gift of abundant life. You are now the recipient of blessings beyond measure. You now have a living hope that can never be taken away from you.

This is the best news I could ever give you.

This is the glory of adoption.

Your adoption.

---

v   1 Peter 1:3-4

chapter 21

VILLAGE *People*

September 25, 2012 was one of my favorite days in Uganda. Not only did I officially become the proud mother of Daughter #4, but my best friend Dianna, along with her husband Josh, arrived in Kampala to begin their own adoption journey with their son, Job. Can you imagine my unhinged joy at having my friend join me in the trenches? When the taxi pulled into our hotel and Dianna got out of the car, I lost my mind. I screamed at the top of my lungs and embraced her as if it had been four years since I'd last seen her, instead of a mere four weeks. I was not alone anymore. I had a friend. An ally. A comrade. A partner in arms. I had Dianna.

We gabbed a mile a minute as I helped her unpack her 26 million suitcases. Like us, Josh and Dianna had brought with them trunks full of medical supplies for Emma's clinic. Like us, they came to Uganda with one-way plane tickets and had no idea when they would be returning home. Like us, they were scared out of their minds. But unlike us, they had a friend to greet them when they arrived in a foreign country and help alleviate their fears.

They had met Job that morning and instantly fell in love with him. He and James played together while the adults emptied out suitcases. I filled them in on our first four weeks in Uganda—the highs and the lows, the beautiful people I'd met, and the breathtaking scenery I'd witnessed. I couldn't wait for them to experience the country I had come to love.

That afternoon, once everyone had time to rest, we hired a taxi to drive us to the mall in Kampala and I directed us to the most American restaurant I had found thus far: Café Javas. Their menu boasted an extensive offering of comfort foods: soups, salads, sandwiches, burgers, French fries, pizza, pasta, and some of the best coffee you'll ever drink. Once I discovered this gem, I frequented it quite often. It was a little taste of home. After dinner, we hired a cab to take us back to the hotel. We were exhausted from the events of the day, but oh so happy to be together.

The next morning, Josh and Dianna set out on a two-day trip to Job's village to begin acquiring the necessary paperwork for his adoption. I happily agreed to keep Job with me for those few days so they could be child-free and maneuver around a bit quicker. That same day, Cathy arrived from her journey to Kabale, carrying with her my newest daughter, Jolie Danielle Akansasira. The sheer elation I experienced holding this baby in my arms, remembering how it felt for her to be taken from me just two nights ago and now knowing she was officially mine forever—it was unreal. By midday, I found myself in my hotel room, alone, surrounded by three tiny Ugandans. The babies God had promised. And I let out a laugh. I was seeing the goodness of God. I was living it in real time.

But you know by now, my season in Uganda was a complete

rollercoaster ride. I couldn't get too comfortable, because I knew how quickly the rug could be pulled out from underneath me and I'd be brought to my knees. This happened to me during naptime that afternoon. It was morning in Texas and Bradley decided to Skype me in with my girls on the car ride to school. Ava and Greta looked so precious in their uniforms. Harper was dressed for ballet class. Their hair was an absolute disaster because daddy was in charge, but nobody cared (including me... kind of). God knows that man was doing the best he could. They all talked at once, telling me about their school projects, soccer teams, new dolls. It was a chatty free-for-all. They were so happy to see my face. All too quickly, they arrived at school and hung up the phone. And I sat at the table in my kitchenette on the other side of the world and bawled my eyes out as they went on with their lives. My God, how I missed my girls and I still didn't know when I would see them again. Sadness overwhelmed me once more.

About 20 minutes into my afternoon cry fest, there was a knock on my hotel room door. It was a mail delivery from my friends Andy and Lauren back in Dallas. The box was filled to the brim with incredibly thoughtful goodies: the cutest clothes for James and Jolie, instant Starbucks packets (what a luxury!), sugar-free sweetener (so very necessary), anti-itch cream (for the mosquito bites all over me), citronella wrist bands (again, mosquitos), a beautiful bracelet and scarf (for me), and a box of Cheerios (for the kids). The timeliness of this delivery was nothing short of miraculous. The Lord knew I needed to be reminded of His love for me. He knew I needed assurance of His provision. He knew I needed confirmation I was still where He wanted me to be. And He used this gift package from my friends as a way of steadying my heart that day.

CREATED FOR COMMUNITY

God often uses other people to carry His message of love to us. He created us for community. We are meant to live life in fellowship with one another. The phrase "it takes a village" isn't in the Bible, but it's rock-solid truth. It does take a village to raise our kids. It does take a village to live this Christian life. It does take a village to walk in love. Because these are hard things to do. And we were never meant to do them alone. So who are your village people? Who are the friends you do life with? Who is your community? Who encourages you? Who holds you accountable? Who provokes you into good works for the Lord? The Bible has a lot to say about living in Christian community:

> And let us consider one another in order to provoke love and good works, not neglecting to gather together, as some are in the habit of doing, but encouraging each other, and all the more as you see the day approaching.
> (Hebrews 10:24-25)

> Carry one another's burdens; in this way you will fulfill the law of Christ. (Galatians 6:2)

Therefore, as God's chosen ones, holy and dearly loved, put on compassion, kindness, humility, gentleness, and patience, bearing with one another and forgiving one another if anyone has a grievance against another. Just as the Lord has forgiven you, so you are also to forgive. Above all, put on love, which is the perfect bond of unity. (Colossians 3:12-14)

A friend loves at all times, and a brother is born for a difficult time. (Proverbs 17:17)

Iron sharpens iron, and one person sharpens another. (Proverbs 27:17)

Love one another deeply as brothers and sisters. Take the lead in honoring one another... Share with the saints in their needs; pursue hospitality... Rejoice with those who rejoice; weep with those who weep. Live in harmony with one another. (Romans 12:10, 13, 15-16)

We are created for community. We are designed for discourse. We are fashioned for friendship. And it takes a village of fellow believers to make this happen. The book of Acts describes the early church in this way:

> Now the entire group of those who believed were of one heart and mind, and no one claimed that any of his possessions was his own, but instead they held everything in common. With great power the apostles were giving testimony to the resurrection of the Lord Jesus, and great grace was on all of them.[i]

The church grew exponentially in number daily under intense persecution. And this didn't happen in large stadiums or crowded sanctuaries or fancy worship centers with slick sound systems. This growth occurred in people's houses. The church met in living rooms, around kitchen tables, in attics and basements. Not in ornate buildings with stained glass and polished pews and gilded steeples.

I currently live in what is commonly called the Bible Belt. My experience with church is limited to that of a megachurch with countless programs, perfectly produced Sunday services, and a well-planned event almost every day of the week. It's all I've known. And that's okay. I was literally raised in this kind of church. I've made deep friendships at these churches that have stayed with me to this day. I've experienced the presence of God at these churches. I've heard the voice of the Lord at these churches. I've matured in my theology at these churches. My kids accepted Jesus as their Savior in these churches. I'm grateful for these churches.

But church was never meant to be merely a place I go on Sundays. Church was always supposed to be part of my identity.

---

i   Acts 4:32-33

I am a Christ-follower. Therefore, *I am the Church*. The Greek word for "church" in the New Testament is *ekklesia*, meaning "those who anywhere—in a city or village—constitute such a company and are united into one body."[12] The key word in this definition is *those*. As in, *those people* are the Church. Not *that place* is the Church.

What does this mean now? For us and for our village? It means that when we take a meal to a sick friend, *we are the Church*. When we show up at the hospital to pray for someone in need, *we are the Church*. When we invite people into our homes to share a meal and uplifting conversation around the dinner table, *we are the Church*. When we send an encouraging email or scripture to a neighbor, *we are the Church*. When we choose to forgive that friend who wronged us, *we are the Church*. When we send a care package to a friend in a foreign country, *we are the Church*. When we care for the widow and the orphan, *we are the Church*. When we share our testimony of God's faithfulness in our lives, *we are the Church*. Church happens in our village, with our people.

Andy and Lauren were part of my village that gloomy afternoon in Kampala. God showed me His love and kindness through their generosity. He showed me He cares for the details of my life through their thoughtfulness. He showed me the great lengths He'll go to bless me through the long-distance delivery of their package. Andy and Lauren were my village. They were the Church.

You want to know something cool? My church family was also my village. While I was in Uganda, countless friends showed up at our house with gifts for my daughters, or hot meals so Bradley wouldn't have to cook. Women came and cleaned my house. Friends helped my mom assemble bunk beds to accommodate our growing family. People assisted with carpool line and shuttling my girls to soccer practice or ballet class. Our church choir stayed late after many Wednesday night rehearsals to pray for me. My church showed up for me. They helped carry my burdens. The church was my village.

Dianna was and is and forevermore will be part of my village. Other than my husband, Dianna is the only person who has firsthand knowledge of what I experienced through this adoption process. We've been in the trenches together. We've cried together, prayed together, fought together, laughed together, struggled together, and grown together for nearly 20 years.

She has her own incredible, awe-inspiring, miracle-filled adoption story. It's very similar to mine, yet wildly different. And it's not mine to tell. But just know that she too has seen the goodness of God. Dianna sharpens me. She's blunt, honest, to the point, and tells it like it is. She doesn't tiptoe around my feelings. She carries my burdens, and I carry hers. She also happens to live directly across the street from me in Dallas. Dianna is in my village (both spiritually and literally) forever.

Find your village people, Friend. Find your community. Find your tribe. If this sounds difficult for you, or if you're isolated and don't know how to even go about this, here is some advice: In order to have a friend, you must first be a friend. Look around you and find someone in need and go help them. Smile at people. Be inquisitive and curious about other's lives. Listen to understand. Serve those around you, like Jesus did. Invite your neighbors to your home for a meal. It's that simple and it's that complicated. Finding your people takes time and energy, but it's oh so worth it. Because God created us for each other. The world needs you. Go be a friend. Go be a village. *Go be the Church.*

chapter 22

Mommy is M.I.A.

At this point, I had been in Uganda for four weeks, and I desperately missed my girls back in Texas. Have I mentioned that yet? I had been away from Ava, Greta, and Harper for an entire month, and I was not doing well. (To put it mildly.) They were on my mind the moment I woke up every morning. I longed for them all day long, constantly looking at the clock in an attempt to keep up with their schedules nine time zones away. They were the last thing I thought of at night. I had insanely vivid dreams of them when I slept. My longing for my daughters was all-consuming. And the longer I stayed in Uganda, the more of their life moments I missed.

I missed the daily rhythm of school. I missed drop-off and pick-up. It was Ava's 2nd grade year and Greta's kindergarten year. Each day was a new adventure. I missed packing their lunchboxes every morning. I knew Ava would eat literally anything I packed for her, but Greta stuck with string cheese, grapes, and goldfish (all three of which were dipped in hummus). I missed book fairs. I missed Rodeo Day. I missed Grandparents Day. Harper was three years old and in our church's Mother's Day Out preschool program two days a week. She still took naps on a monogrammed mat at school and was learning to go teetee and poopoo on the potty. (Silver lining: I didn't potty train my third child. Thank goodness my mom did that for me while I was away. Parenting win.) Harper preferred a Lunchable and a mandarin orange at school. She would peel her orange and line up all the segments in two perfect columns and eat one and a time. (Her OCD showed itself early.) I missed oohing and aahing over every project or craft that came home in their backpacks, then secretly throwing them in the trash when they weren't looking. (If this isn't your testimony, please don't tell my children.)

I missed Ava's and Greta's soccer games every Saturday. Ava showed early signs of elevated skills on the field. She played Forward and scored often. She hustled, worked hard, gave it her all, and had zero tolerance for any teammates who didn't match her efforts. Greta, on the other hand, only played soccer because all her best friends were on the team. Soccer games were social hour. She became an expert at cartwheels during soccer season, while mostly playing defense and hanging out by the goal. She perfected her twirl and collected bouquets of dandelion weeds from the grass beneath her. She lived for the snacks.

I missed Harper's first few months of ballet. She took dance class with Dianna's daughter, Hallie, who had been Harper's best friend from birth. I missed the little pink shoes, the tutus, and the leotards. I missed seeing her little chunky feet standing in first position. I missed watching her giggle with her friend and cheering her on while she danced. Many pictures of Harper in her tutu were sent to me while I was in Uganda. And I would smile through my tears every time.

I missed our Wednesday night family dinners at Chick-

Fil-A before church activities. We were regulars at this particular establishment, and the lovely employees (Josh and Ivy) knew our order by heart. They would help me get our table set up with placemats, napkins, ketchup, and juice boxes. After dinner, we would then travel across the street to church and disperse to our respective events: children's choir for the girls followed by AWANA club, and adult choir rehearsal for me and Bradley. This was our Wednesday night routine for more than a decade. And I missed it.

I missed bath time and bedtime with my girls. I missed reading *Fancy Nancy* books and singing our favorite songs together while they lay in bed. I missed trying not to laugh out loud when their bedtime prayers were hilarious. "Dear God, I have a booger nose," is one of Harper's classics. I missed collapsing on the couch once they were all asleep and watching TV with Bradley. I missed taking a relaxing bubble bath before crawling into bed and falling fast sleep, then waking up to do it all over again the next day.

But the thing that hurt the worst? The event that dumped the most salt in my gaping wounds? I missed Greta's sixth birthday on October 6th. Having left for Uganda at the end of August, it never even dawned on me I could possibly still be in Africa come October. As I've stated, we were expecting to be in-country for only three weeks. Eventually, I realized I wouldn't be home for this monumental experience. It was the insult to my injury. Bradley was back in Texas by this time, and my village kicked into high gear to make sure Greta was celebrated. She partnered up with her two best friends, Ella and Ava Grace, for a cowgirl party, complete with pony rides and bounce houses. My inbox and Facebook feed were flooded with photos from this shindig, smiles on every face.

I was Skyped in to the party her kindergarten teacher threw for her at school. I watched as she stood in a chair with a "Happy Birthday" hat perched on her head, smiling sheepishly while the kids sang out of tune then crammed cupcakes in their mouths. Bradley and my mother took the girls to the *American Girl* store in Dallas and let Greta pick out her very first American Girl doll, along with all the accessories her heart desired. It was an over-the-top occasion.

Greta may say it was her favorite birthday ever. Her memories of this time are only good. But I was dead on the inside as I watched these events take place from the other side of the world. Each photo, video, and smile I saw on my screen reminded me I was not there.

WRESTLING WITH GOD

I missed a significant amount of my girls' lives. And they knew it. They felt it. They realized I was doing something that most other mommies have never done: I left my children for weeks and weeks at a time with no idea as to when I would return home. My girls were aware of how strange this was, and they did not make it through this season unscathed. My absence affected them each in different ways. The short-term and long-term consequences of my time away in Uganda have been significant, some of which we are still dealing with ten years later. Anxiety, depression, fear of separation, fear of abandonment—these are some of the residual effects my daughters have experienced due to my absence. So I can't keep myself from asking…

Did my stubborn obedience to the Lord ruin my kids' lives?

I asked myself this question while I was in Uganda, and I've asked it about a million times since. Why? Because God keeps asking me and Bradley to do some pretty crazy things. And our kids are strapped into this roller-coaster ride with us, whether they like it or not.

Is following Jesus harming my children? Are we serving the Lord at their expense? Did we make a mistake when we chose to surrender our lives to God's plan?

Friend, I have struggled with this for *years*. I have stepped into the wrestling ring with God and we have duked it out over this subject. Round after round after round. We have grappled. We have put in the work together. Because I am aware that it can absolutely appear as if we've ruined our kids' lives. And to some, it may seem like the juice wasn't worth the squeeze. Or that the ends don't justify the means.

But in all my wrestling and struggling and grappling, God has been ever so gentle and patient with me. He has never been offended by my questions. He has never been put off by my worry over my kids. Instead, God met me where I was, in the middle of my strife, and built my faith in His goodness. God has lovingly taken me through some very dark seasons and taught me how to trust Him not only *with* my children, but *for* my children. He has assured me over and over again, and I believe this to my bones: *God's plan for me and Bradley is also His plan for our children.* Please allow me to elaborate here:

- God's calling on our lives is also His calling on our kids' lives.

- God's anointing on our lives is also His anointing on our kids' lives.
- God's assignment for our lives is also His assignment for our kids' lives.
- God's covering over our lives is also His covering over our kids' lives.
- God's grace for our lives is also His grace for our kids' lives.
- God's strength for our lives is also His strength for our kids' lives.

In other words, as long as these small humans are under our roof and in our care, God's plan for us as parents is also His plan for our children.

And it gets better: God's plan for us collectively as a family is also His plan for us individually as His sons and daughters. I'll unpack this a bit more. God had something specific He wanted to accomplish in Harper's life by teaching her to trust other people while I was in Uganda. God had something specific He wanted to do in Ava's life by allowing her to experience those weeks and weeks while I was thousands of miles away. God had something specific He wanted to do for Greta, so He let her see the family of God in action, supporting her and celebrating her while I was gone. God had something specific for James and Jolie, for which He paved the way, brick by brick, miracle by miracle. God was accomplishing His individual plan for each of us as He accomplished His grand plan for our family. And He wasn't stressed out in the slightest. This wasn't too difficult for Him.

GOOD NEWS FOR EVERY MOM

One of the most significant and comforting Bible verses that has profoundly ministered to me is Isaiah 40:11. It's such good news. I still read it and weep.

> He will feed his flock like a shepherd.
> He will carry the lambs in his arms,
> holding them close to his heart.
> He will gently lead the mothers
> with their young. (ESV)

Is this not a breath of fresh air to your lungs? Working mom? Single mom? Mom with more kids than she can keep track of? Friend, let this wash over you today. The God who calls you to fulfill His assignments (big and small) loves your children more than you could ever imagine. You can absolutely rest on the promises found in this verse:

- *God will provide for your family.* "He will feed his flock like a shepherd." He will make sure you have everything you need to accomplish your purpose. He will equip you to do every good work He has called you to. He will enable your stubborn obedience. You will lack nothing.
- *God will protect your children.* "He will carry the lambs in his arms, holding them close to his heart." Did you read that clearly??? As you stubbornly follow God on the path where He leads you, *He is carrying your children.* Not you. You were never meant to carry your kids through this life. You're not strong enough. Hand them over to the Good Shepherd. Let Him be in control

of the consequences of your obedience. God can handle it. He loves your kids more than you do.

- *God will empower you, Mom.* "He will gently lead the mothers with their young." He knows this life is hard. He knows the weight you carry as a mother. He knows you're exhausted from holding it all together. He knows you question every decision. He knows you beat yourself up over every choice you make, and how you never feel like you're doing a good enough job. He knows the guilt you carry. He knows your struggles. And with more grace than you could ever imagine, He gently leads you, sweet Mother, as you make decisions for your children, as you serve your family, as you do the holy work of parenting, as you stubbornly obey Him. He's gently leading you. And He's filling you with His power to get the job done.

God has our kids. And He's leading us moms with so much grace, kindness, and gentleness. His plan for all of us (including our children) is specific and good. Is it possible we will be throwing our kids into the lion's den when we follow God wherever He leads? Yes. But our Good Shepherd is also one heck of a lion tamer. Our children will have a front-row seat to the unlimited power and protection our glorious God offers to those who belong to Him.

Could our children be thrown into a fiery furnace when we relentlessly obey God? Probably. But our Savior has a way of showing up in the fire and bringing them out, unharmed and unsinged. We won't be able to find the faintest bit of smoke on them when we smell their blessed heads. When our kids watch their parents follow Jesus at any cost, they will be witnesses to the glory of God. They will know that God is who He says He is, because their parents have shown them. And this will become part of their testimony. This will be part of their story. God is carrying our babies *close to His heart* along the path as He leads us. You can trust Him. God has your kids, Friend. Keep following Him.

chapter 23

WHITE FLAGS AND
Roadblocks

Along this journey, God set up significant mile markers confirming and affirming our call to adopt, one of which turned out to be very full circle. It took place while we were awaiting James' second hearing at Family Court in Uganda. It was a concert. But before I give you any more details, I need to take you back in time seven months, to March 2012. Back to when God first called us to adopt.

LONDON FOG

When God spoke to us regarding bringing two children into our home through adoption, Bradley and I initially kept the news to ourselves. There were so many unknowns: *When will this happen? Where will we be adopting from? How old will the children be?* These were all questions we weren't prepared to answer, so we kept our new assignment close to the chest until God revealed more of His plan.

At this same exact time, Bradley was writing and preparing for the pinnacle of his musical career. He had written a masterpiece—his opus—a timeless, classic Christmas album, including a 22-minute original piece entitled "The Nativity Symphony." It was a fully scored and narrated account of the birth of our Savior. And in March of 2012, we traveled to London, England, for Bradley to record this project with the London Symphony at Abbey Road Studios, in the same room where the soundtracks for *Star Wars, Harry Potter,* and *Indiana Jones* were recorded. This was the opportunity of his lifetime. I could write four chapters on this experience alone. It was amazingly satisfying to watch my husband thrive in his gifts and talents. He was in his element in every way. The recording session was an absolute success.

After Bradley's studio dates, we stayed in England for a week to vacation and explore. I remember visiting some incredible places like Big Ben, Harrod's, Westminster Abbey, and Buckingham Palace, all while being more than slightly distracted by the new revelation we had received from the Lord regarding adoption. It felt as if I was floating through London, my mind in a fog. On Sunday, we decided to take a day trip to the town of Brighton, on the southern coast of England overlooking the English Channel. The train ride south was spectacular, meandering through small villages and rolling hills. We spent the day sightseeing, walking along the coast, and feasting on fresh fish and chips. We were thrilled to discover a church in town was holding evening services, and we decided to attend. This church happened to be home to well-known worship leader/songwriter Matt Redman. And Matt Redman happened to be leading worship that very night.

The church was centuries old. It was small and humble, yet beautiful in its ornate details and stained glass. Instead of chairs, the nearly 100 congregants in attendance sat on plush pillows on the floor. The environment felt intimate and reverent. Matt Redman came out holding his guitar and lead us in worship. We sang many songs that had been familiar to us for years: "Here I Am to Worship," "10,000 Reasons," and "Here for You," to name a few. But the atmosphere shifted when he played a specific song—a new one that hadn't yet been released. A song called "White Flag." It felt as if it had been written specifically for Bradley and me at that moment:

> Here on this holy ground,
> You made a way for peace.
> Laying your body down,
> You took our rightful place.
> This freedom song is marching on.
> We raise our white flag,
> We surrender all to you, all for you.
> We raise our white flag,
> The war is over,
> Love has come, your love has won.[13]

We were in a season where we felt called, but still had so many unanswered questions. We knew we had a grand assignment, but we didn't yet have all the details. We said "yes" to God without fully knowing what we had said "yes" to. We were in the beautiful tension of surrender. And there, in an obscure Anglican Church in Brighton, England, God confirmed that He expected our complete surrender through this entire process, from beginning to end. And we conceded. With our hands lifted high on that Sunday night, Bradley and I waved our white flags of surrender to the Lord. We would follow Him, no matter the cost, even if we didn't have all the answers.

PASSION KAMPALA

Let's jump back to October 2012 in Kampala, the days between James' court hearings. (Are you with me?) Our progress was stalled until we received full legal guardianship of James. I found myself, yet again, having to wait on the Lord.

Emma caught wind of an event taking place at Makarere University in Kampala. Renowned evangelist Louie Giglio's Passion Conference was on world tour and made a stop in the heart of Uganda. Emma, Sarah, Josh, Dianna, and I bought tickets and made our way to the campus' vast red dirt field, filled with thousands of young Ugandans hungry for the Lord. The air was electric with the sound of praise, as Chris Tomlin and Christy Nockels led us in worship.

This evening took me on a wild ride of extreme emotions. Initially, I was glad to be in the presence of God. I felt safe. But the familiarity of the music and the faces onstage quickly made me feel a deep sense of homesickness. I was ready to be singing these songs back in Texas. My sadness then turned to anger as it dawned on me that all the Americans on stage were free to go home whenever they wanted. They weren't stuck in this country like I was. They weren't in a holding pattern. They could sing their little songs and preach their little sermons, then hop on a plane and go back to their families. And I was stuck there, still unsure of when I would get to leave. In that moment, I felt like a hostage.

Then I heard Chris Tomlin say, "We've got a new song to play for you tonight. You may know it. It's a song of surrender and freedom!" He played the intro to "White Flag" and the crowd joined in declaring, "We surrender all to you, all for you!" And immediately my mind flashed back to that quaint cathedral in England, where we heard this song for the first time. I remembered how Bradley and I lifted our hands and yielded our lives to God. We didn't have all the answers then, but we said "yes" anyways. We entered into the beautiful tension of surrender. And here I was, still in that tension. Yet, I now had mile marker after mile marker of God's faithfulness behind me. I had seen Him work on my behalf time and time again. He had proven Himself trustworthy and true. There was safety in my surrender.

All these thoughts flooded my mind as I sang, and I felt my hands raise in submission, once again. God had brought me full circle with this song. I was standing in the "unknown place" I had trusted Him for, seven months prior, back in England. I had one answered prayer in the form of Jolie, and another answered prayer on the way with James. I was witnessing the fruit of my surrender. I was in the center of God's plan for my life. I was seeing Romans 12:1 in action: "Therefore, brothers and sisters, in view of the mercies of God, I urge you to present your bodies as a living sacrifice, holy and pleasing to God; this is your true worship." My stubborn obedience was my worship.

My white flag was still lifted high.

CRAZY JENNY FROM THE BLOCK

The next morning brought alarming news. We learned Jolie's entire adoption process was being sabotaged by none other than Jenny, the orphanage director. (Do you remember Crazy Jenny from a few chapters back?) The flash of favor she had for us in her office that day in Kisoro had disappeared. She was now on the prowl, interfering with paperwork, slowing down procedures, and calling up government officials in an attempt to block our progress, even though Jolie was legally and officially ours. Jenny's meddling was illegal.

At this point, we should've had Jolie's entire file from the court delivered to us in order to proceed with applying for her passport. But the file was nowhere to be found. Jenny's interference had made its way all the way up to Kisoro's Resident District Commissioner (RDC), the man in charge of signing her passport form. Without his signature, we couldn't obtain her passport. And we couldn't leave the country. We had hit another major roadblock.

To complicate matters even more, Uganda's 50th Jubilee celebration was the following week. The country was celebrating the 50th anniversary of their independence from British rule. It was anticipated to be the party of the century. All government offices would be closed *the entire week*. Kisoro was a 14-hour drive away. There was no realistic way we could drive out there and muscle our way through this. I'm not exaggerating when I say I looked into chartering a prop plane to fly me out to Kisoro to personally handle this situation. I was ready for a flight and a fight. Our bank account, however, wasn't ready to dish out that kind of money.

READY FOR WAR

This felt like a deliberate attack. Warfare was taking place all around me and had been for weeks. By this time, I knew who my enemy was, and it wasn't Crazy Jenny. It was the devil himself. I was living out Ephesians 6:12 in real time: "For our struggle is not against flesh and blood, but against the... cosmic powers of this darkness." Satan was coming after me and my children. Satan was trying to sabotage my adoption. Satan was meddling in my business. And I was furious. He was messing with the wrong girl. I was ready for battle.

I didn't fly to Kisoro that day. Instead, I went back to the first sermon I preached at Passion Christian Assembly on 2 Chronicles 20. I remembered how King Jehoshaphat led the armies of Israel to turn their eyes upon the Lord when they were surrounded on all sides. I remembered how the Israelites shouted and worshiped God, and their praise confounded their enemies, so much so that their enemies turned on one another and destroyed each other. I remembered their battle strategy. And I marched up to my room and blared praise music and sang at the top of my lungs. Worship was my weapon. Lifting my voice confounded my adversary. I sang until my voice quit on me. But my hands and my feet still worked, so I clapped and stomped and danced my way to victory. Satan wouldn't win. He couldn't have my children.

That afternoon, Emma received a phone call from Ezra, the kind gentleman who served as the orphanage's senior director. Earlier that day, he had taken it upon himself to speak with the RDC directly and plead our case. Ezra said he felt the presence of God with him as they spoke. The RDC did not sign Jolie's passport file; he had a better idea. He would be traveling to Kampala for Jubilee the following week and would bring the file himself. He wanted to meet with me personally and hear my story and meet Jolie. Something totally unheard of from an RDC. I eagerly agreed, knowing that this was God's handiwork. This was His victory. This battle was won. And all I had to do was sing.

Roadblocks happen. We all have a Crazy Jenny in our life. (If you don't have a Crazy Jenny in your life, chances are *you might be the Crazy Jenny.* I say this with love.) We all have people or circumstances that come against the assignment God has for us. We all have a thorn in our side of some sort. We all face opposition. Because—hear me, Friend—when you say "yes" to whatever God has for you and make up your mind to stubbornly obey Him, *you will have a target on your back.* Satan doesn't waste his time on apathetic Christians. Lazy, lukewarm believers don't have his attention. He has his eye on those of us who are doing the thing. Fighting the fight. Walking the walk. Willing to pay the cost. Waving our white flags in surrender to Jesus. He can't stand us. And he will do whatever it takes to try to destroy us. He's smart. He's shrewd. And he just flat out ticks me off.

BUT THE VICTORY IS ALREADY OURS.

Do you hear me? Because I'm attempting to shout at you through the caps lock button of my computer. Your roadblock is not a dead end. Your Crazy Jenny doesn't have the final say. The thorn in your side does not have to paralyze you. The victory is already yours through the death, burial, and resurrection of Jesus Christ. Romans 8:37 tells us that "in all these things we are more than conquerors through him who loved us." Jesus tells us Himself in John 16:33, "You will have suffering in this world. Be courageous! I have conquered the world." We are more than conquerors because the God we serve has already conquered. It's done. The war is won. Hallelujah.

Stay in the battle, Friend. You may have a real enemy, but you have a Mighty God. And greater is the God that is within you than the enemy that is in the world.[i] Stubborn obedience will undoubtedly put a target on your back, but your Savior has encircled you and placed His hand on you.[ii] Roadblocks will appear, but your Protector will not allow your foot to slip.[iii] Keep presenting yourself as a living sacrifice. This is the act of worship that will confound your enemy.[iv] Keep praising. Keep worshiping. Keep believing. Keep trusting. Keep obeying. Keep waving your white flag in surrender to Jesus and watch as your enemy is destroyed while you sing.

---

i   1 John 4:4
ii   Psalm 139:5
iii   Psalm 121:3
iv   Romans 12:1

chapter 24

Akanonda

The day finally arrived for James' second court hearing. I paid the fare for Agatha (the woman who found James), Issah (the Manafwa county probation officer), and the Muzetati Police Chief to be bussed to Kampala and be in attendance. They would each give a firsthand account of the facts surrounding James' story. Their testimony should remove all doubt as to the validity of his adoptability. And since Bradley and I had already met with this judge, there would be no reason for further delay with his ruling. We should be granted legal guardianship immediately. Against my better judgment, I had high hopes for this day at court.

LET'S TRY THAT AGAIN

I left Jolie at the hotel with Dianna and dressed James in the best clothes I had for him. We filed into the downtown courthouse waiting room with Emma, George, and our three visitors from the east. We made ourselves comfortable in our chairs, and we waited. And waited. And waited. I got up to use the bathroom and came and sat back in my seat and waited some more. We waited for more than two hours. A clerk finally came and informed us the judge would not be seeing us today, and we were instructed to come back tomorrow. I posted on my Facebook page that day: "I am never going to leave Africa."

The following morning, I once again left Jolie at the hotel with Dianna and dressed James in the exact same outfit. The usual suspects filed into the courthouse waiting room. And we waited some more. Apparently, I hadn't yet fully learned my lesson on how to wait for the Lord because He kept giving me opportunities for growth in this area. This time, we waited in that holding room for three hours before seeing the judge.

When we finally made our way to the judge's chambers, he took his time and was diligent with his questioning of everyone in attendance. Most of the conversations were beyond my comprehension due to the language barrier, but I was studying everybody's body language to the best of my ability. Agatha was at ease and spoke freely and easily when questioned. Likewise with Issah and the Muzetati Police Chief. The judge appeared sincere with his comments and remarks. He once again questioned me (in English), wanting to make sure I had full disclosure of James' medical history, which I assured him I had. When he seemed satisfied with our answers, he instructed me to come back the following Friday (during Jubilee) to receive his ruling. This was a full week away. The delayed ruling was disappointing. But after that second hearing, I was more confident than ever James would be ours. I simply had to wait. Yet again.

The week of Jubilee passed slowly, but I was determined to soak in all the Ugandan culture I could. I stayed glued to the TV during naptime, watching the parades, concerts, and festivities.

Dianna and I took the kids out to various markets, stocking up on souvenirs and native artwork. At this point, Josh and Dianna had completed their court hearing for Job's case, and Josh had returned home to Texas to be with their kids. We enjoyed exploring new restaurants every evening and finding new parks and playgrounds for the kids to roam. It was Dianna and me against the world.

THE BOY IS MINE

October 12, 2012, the date of the judge's ruling, arrived. Once again, I found myself in the judge's office, clutching my baby boy. I'll never forget that kind man sitting behind his desk, looking over the top rim of his glasses, and quietly saying, "The boy is yours." The boy was mine. James was mine. I had a son. This was the Lord's doing.

I immediately called Bradley and congratulated him on having more testosterone in our house. I could hear his tears through the phone. As soon as I arrived back at our hotel, I ran and told Dianna, flinging my arms around her and crying on her shoulder. She cried with me. God did what He said he would do. He answered my prayers. He kept His promises. I was now officially the mother of five children. At the age of 29. Jesus, take the wheel.

NEW NAME

Remember in Chapter 10, when I told you Agatha had named my son Mumwata James? *Mumwata* means "trash, dumped, thrown out, abandoned." I told you I hated that name from the moment I heard it. It rubbed me the wrong way. I told you that everywhere my son went, that horrible word was spoken over his life. He heard it every day. And I told you, come hell or high water, we would be changing our boy's name.

My son's new name is James William Akanonda Knight. As I mentioned, "James" is my mother's maiden name, so he had an automatic tie to my side of the family. We gave him the middle name of "William," which is Bradley's mother's maiden name, giving him a connection to the paternal side. And we gave him the Ugandan name of *Akanonda*, meaning "God has chosen me." With one sentence from a judge's mouth, James's life was forever changed. He was abandoned. Now he's chosen. He was an orphan. Now he's a son. He was alone. Now he belongs.

This is the glory of adoption.

CHOSEN

James's story is my story. It's your story, too. We were lost, abandoned, tossed out, discarded by our sin. Sin isn't a popular subject to speak about or write about these days, but that doesn't change the fact it exists and we were born into it. Sin is defined as "an offense against the law of God."[14] And this sin separated us from God. The Bible does not mince words:

> But your iniquities are separating you from your
> God, and your sins have hidden his face from you
> so that he does not listen. (Isaiah 59:2)

> For all have sinned and fall short of the glory of
> God. (Romans 3:23)

> If we say, "We have no sin," we are deceiving
> ourselves, and the truth is not in us. (1 John 1:8)

The Bible goes on to tell us the punishment for our sin is death, which equates to complete abandonment and separation from God.[i] Because of our sinful nature, we were, in essence, trash.

But God.

He came searching for you. He came seeking you out. He found you. And He chose you. Even while you were still knee-deep in sin. Romans 5:8 says, "But God proves his own love for us in that while we were still sinners, Christ died for us." You were abandoned. You were thrown out. But God had His eye on you. And He sent His only Son to step into time and shrink Himself to fit within our humanity. He lived a perfect, sinless life and was crucified on a cross, bearing the weight of the world's sin. He was buried and came back to life three days later, forever defeating death. And He did all this in order to call you *chosen.*

Because of this great sacrifice, you are now adopted into the family of God. Paul paints a beautiful picture of this truth in Galatians:

> When the time came to completion, God sent
> his Son, born of a woman, born under the law,
> to redeem those under the law, so that we might
> receive adoption as sons. And because you are

---

i   Romans 6:23

now sons, God sent the Spirit of his Son into your hearts, crying "Abba, Father!" So you are no longer a slave but a son, and if a son, then God has made you an heir. (Galatians 4:4-7)

You and I are now grafted into God's family, just like James and Jolie are grafted into our family. We belong to each other forever. What are the privileges that come with being a child in the Knight family? I'll list a few:

- When my kids are hungry, I feed them.
- When my kids are sick, I take them to the doctor and give them medicine to heal them.
- When my kids are dirty, I clean them.
- When my kids are lonely, I stay by their side.
- When my kids are sad, I comfort them.
- When my kids are happy, I laugh with them.
- When my kids are attempting to accomplish a big task, I cheer them on and give them all the resources they need to be successful.
- When my kids are exposed, I cover them.
- When my kids are in danger, I protect them.
- When my kids are little beasts, I love them.

This is a pretty great list of privileges that come with being a part of our imperfect, messed up family. Think about how much more God loves you and has to offer you. This includes all the above and infinitely more. As His child, you now have total access to all He is and all He has. Because you are His heir, you have access to His power, His salvation, His deliverance, His joy, His grace, His peace, His provision, His protection, His mercy, His love, His kindness, His goodness. And none of these benefits ever run out. He's on your side forever. What a wealth of riches!

NEW FAMILY

Before I ever began writing this book, I knew this specific chapter would be the most important one I wrote. Because it's an invitation for you to join the Family. It's an invitation for you to open your heart to the adoption that awaits you. If you've made it this far in our story, you know we're believers in Jesus. I have not been ambiguous about this in any way. We're die-hard, sold-out Jesus freaks. And proud of it. Maybe you've never had an experience with Him. Maybe you're unsure if you're a part of His family. Maybe you don't know where you stand. You can be sure today. You can be sure right now.

It all starts with acknowledging your shortcomings. Admitting where you've failed. And knowing you need help. You must confess your sins.[ii] There is no shame in this. We were all born lost.[iii] There's no judgment or condemnation here. Love is waiting for you.

Once you've recognized you can't make it on your own, it's time to look to Jesus. You must believe He is who He says He is. That He is God's son. That He was born of a virgin and lived a perfect life. That He bore your sin on a cross and took it with Him to the grave. That He was raised to life three days later and is alive today. That He ascended to heaven and hangs out at the right hand of God, praying for you day and night. Believing in

---

ii   Romans 10:9
iii   Romans 3:23

this good news is your path to adoption. It's the way to glorious eternal life in heaven.[iv]

When you're ready to be adopted, all it takes is a simple prayer. And if that intimidates you, it's okay. Prayer is simply talking to God and giving Him space to speak to you. You don't have to be comfortable with prayer right now. I'll help you. I've written a simple prayer that you're free to recite, out loud or in your heart. These are not magical words. There's nothing special about this prayer. The change happens when you pray with a sincere heart. If you're ready to take the next step, pray this prayer:

> Heavenly Father, I don't know why you chose to love me, but I'm so glad you did. I'm ready to be part of your Family. I realize I'm a sinner and I can't make it through this life on my own. I need a Father. I believe you sent your son Jesus to die in my place and bear my sins. Jesus, I believe you are alive today and I want you to be Lord of my life. Thank you for loving me. Thank you for choosing me. Thank you for adopting me. In Jesus's name, I pray all these things. Amen.

If you prayed that prayer just now, I get the honor of being the first to say, "WELCOME TO THE FAMILY!!!!" You probably can't hear it, but there's a party being thrown in your honor in heaven right this very minute. And it's wild.

There are some important next steps to take, the first of which is to tell somebody about your decision—a trusted friend,

---

iv   Romans 10:13

family member, or pastor. I would also love to hear from you personally! You can contact me via my website and let me know of your adoption. It would bless me! Next, you need to connect with some of your new brothers and sisters. There's a great big family waiting to meet you! I encourage you to find a local church that preaches the Bible and worships the Lord. It doesn't have to be grand or fancy. Get plugged in and find your village. Your presence is so needed.

You did it, Friend. You made the best decision of your life. Your life has been changed forever. You have a new name, a new identity, a new purpose. God has a good plan for your life. You are loved. You are cherished. You are chosen.

Welcome to the family of God.

chapter 25

JESUS, BE A *Passport*

I had been in Uganda for seven weeks by now. I was officially the mother of two Ugandan babies. By God's grace, I accomplished what I set out to do, and I had my eye on the prize: the departure gate at Entebbe Airport. I was ready to get the heck out of Africa. What I wasn't prepared for, however, was the fight still ahead of me. Looking back, I now view this entire experience as a pregnancy of sorts. And my labor pains were about to get exponentially worse before we were delivered.

HOTEL HEAVEN

For nearly the entire time we were in Uganda, we stayed at a hotel near Emma's house and clinic in the outskirts of Kampala. Every meeting we had at court or Immigration or the US Embassy required at least a 45-minute drive both ways. For this last stretch, I knew I needed to be in the heart of the city. Close proximity to all these government buildings was necessary. And I aimed high. There was a beautiful Sheraton Hotel in the downtown district I had dreamed about from the first week we arrived in August. The nightly price was extremely high, much more than we could afford. So, I quietly posted one sentence on Facebook: "Anybody have hotel reward points they'd be willing to donate?" Within hours, God's people showed up. I had more points than I could've possibly used, and my room was booked at the Sheraton. Dianna put out the same request and was able to book a room next to mine. We were moving on up.

If those last few weeks in Uganda felt like labor, then my room at the Sheraton was my epidural. It eased my pain. It soothed my spirit. It felt a little bit like heaven on earth. I walked into the lobby, immediately greeted by a presence I hadn't felt in weeks: Air Conditioning. My double queen room had a balcony overlooking the immaculately manicured gardens and sparkling pool. The beds were plush and (miraculously!) devoid of mosquito nets. The bathroom had a large soaking tub, perfect for relaxing after I put the babies down at night. The restaurant felt upscale, featuring an extensive menu of familiar dishes. There was room service, laundry service, and housekeeping service. The hotel featured a private playground, for the exclusive use of their tiniest guests. And, best of all, it was a five-minute drive to all relevant government buildings. God knew I was weary. He knew I was ready to leave. And He also knew I would need a shot in the arm to keep me in the fight until the end. The Sheraton was good medicine.

PASSPORT PANDEMONIUM

Before I could apply for immigrant visas at the US Embassy, my babies needed passports. We had submitted James' paperwork to Immigration three weeks prior, hoping to get a jump start on the process. On the Friday of Jubilee week, I met with the Resident District Commissioner (RDC) from Kisoro to obtain Jolie's file and answer any questions he had. I was unnecessarily apprehensive about meeting this man. He held the final key to my return flight home. And he was an absolute delight. He asked me questions about my family, my faith, our life back in Texas, and how my new children were adjusting. He was genuinely interested in our story and happily signed all the passport forms we needed. Before we parted ways, he prayed over me. I will never forget the kindness of the RDC.

Once we had Jolie's documents in hand, we drove straight to the immigration office to get them submitted. I inquired about James' passport status and was told there was a "mix-up" that delayed his information from being processed, but that they were "looking into it" and would push it through immediately. I was instructed to return the following Monday to pick up their passports. I happily spent the weekend relaxing at my beautiful hotel.

I was at the immigration office first thing Monday morning. As soon as I had the passports in hand, I could schedule our visa hearing at the US Embassy and book our flights home! When I arrived at Immigration, I found the officer in charge of our case and asked for my children's passports, as promised. He gave me a puzzled look and said, "They're not ready." The Immigration Commissioner decided to go out of town at the last minute, and *he was the only person in entire the country with the authority to issue passports.* And he wouldn't be returning to the office until Thursday. "You've got to be kidding me" came out of my mouth. Which was ironic because Ugandans don't understand this phrase. I hung my head in defeat, grabbed my children, and we made our way back to our air-conditioned hotel.

That afternoon, while my kids napped in their shared queen bed, I received a call from George. Things had taken a turn for the worse. The Immigration Office decided to put a STOP on all passports issued for Legal Guardianship cases, including ours. Meaning, it was now impossible for me to fly home with my babies. I stepped out onto my beautiful balcony and bawled my eyes out. All this work for nothing. Going home felt so close, yet so very far away.

George, however, was not yet ready to tuck his tail and run away. Ever the lawyer, he still had fight left in him and wasn't prepared to accept "no" for an answer. After a lengthy discussion the following day, we decided George would meet with the Immigration Commissioner when he returned to the office on Thursday, and personally plead our case. I would stay in my hotel room and pray him through it.

Thursday came, and I was a ball of nerves all day long. I'm pretty sure I spent most of the morning on the toilet, and the rest of the day bouncing between fervent prayer and stress eating. Dianna did her best to distract me. We took the kids to the playground, enjoyed a leisurely lunch, and returned to our rooms to put the kids down for naptime. My phone stayed glued to my hand all day long. I checked it every 60 seconds to see if I had missed any calls. Around 1:30, I finally felt it vibrate in my hand. I quietly stepped out onto my balcony and answered it. George had called to inform me the Immigration Commissioner was in a meeting that had lasted all morning and George had not yet seen him. I went back inside my room and kept praying. At

3:30, I looked down at my phone. Still no call from George. I felt my heart sink. This felt like the end.

At 5:30, I decided to Skype Bradley and let him know things didn't go our way today. I still hadn't heard from George and, by now, the Immigration Office was closed. We had some tough decisions to make. While I was filling Bradley in on the day's events, I heard a knock on my door. It was Emma. He had come to tell me that George was successful. The Immigration Commissioner had mercy on our case and signed off on both James' and Jolie's passports. We would have them in hand the following Monday. I hugged Emma and wept on his shoulder. Bradley wept, as well, on the other side of the screen. I was so grateful he was virtually present to hear the good news directly! Dianna and I took the kids to a celebratory dinner at our hotel that night. We had a reason to party.

The next morning, George and Emma made the decision to visit the Immigration Office once again to follow up and confirm the progress of our passports. Jolie's file was in processing, but James' file had mysteriously disappeared. Because nothing in that office was processed digitally, everything was done manually on paper. A missing passport file meant an impossible-to-process passport. The man in charge of James' case was not in the office that day. (Of course.) George and Emma would have to come back on Monday to meet with him. I cried myself to sleep in my high thread-count sheets that night.

A CALL TO ENDURANCE

Are you weary yet, Friend? Has putting yourself inside my story exhausted you? Are you over this whole thing already? Because I was. My God, I was tired. I was tired of praying. I was tired of worshiping. I was tired of crying. I was tired of working. I was tired of obeying. From my point of view, I had done literally everything God had asked of me. I followed Him. I surrendered to Him. I obeyed Him. And yet I was still being knocked down at every turn. I was still being beat up. I was still being pressed. It felt as if absolutely nothing was going my way. And I was tired of it. I was tired of laboring.

Stubborn obedience will eventually exhaust you. It will take you to the end of yourself. It will drain your strength. You will more than likely feel like giving up. Stubborn obedience calls for perseverance and endurance.

We've learned a lot from the apostle Paul through the pages of my journey. He knew what it was to be exhausted. He knew what it meant to persevere for the cause of Christ. In many of his letters to the early church, this was reflected in his writing:

> Let us not grow tired of doing good, for we will reap at the proper time if we don't give up. (Galatians 6:9)

> … being strengthened with all power, according to his glorious might, so that you may have great endurance and patience… (Colossians 1:11)

> Rejoice in hope, be patient in affliction, be persistent in prayer. (Romans 12:12)

> He will repay each one according to his works: eternal life to those who by persistence in doing good seek glory, honor, and immortality.
> (Romans 2:6-7)

The writer of Hebrews also knew about endurance:

> So don't throw away your confidence, which has a great reward. For you need endurance, so that after you have done God's will, you may receive what was promised. (Hebrews 10:35-36)

> ... Let us run with endurance the race that lies before us, keeping our eyes on Jesus, the pioneer and perfecter of our faith. For the joy that lay before him, he endured the cross, despising the shame, and sat down at the right hand of the throne of God. (Hebrews 12:1-2)

This Christian walk is hard. It's a long road. The highs and the lows are extreme, and they can happen abruptly. We are called to endure until the end. We are instructed to forget what is behind us and press forward to what is ahead, pursuing the prize promised by God's heavenly call in Christ Jesus.[i] We are commanded to finish strong. But guess what? We're not expected to do this in our own strength. There's no way we ever possibly could. Again, we look to Paul:

---

i   Philippians 3:13-14

> But he said to me, "My grace is sufficient for you, for my power is perfected in weakness." Therefore, I will most gladly boast all the more about my weaknesses, so that Christ's power may reside in me. So I take pleasure in weaknesses, insults, hardships, persecutions, and in difficulties, for the sake of Christ. For when I am weak, then I am strong. (2 Corinthians 12:9-10)

Christ's power lives in us. It's Jesus who gives us the fortitude to finish well. It's God who empowers us to do the thing. We were never meant to run this race in our own strength. It always has been and forevermore will be, Jesus. He told us Himself, "Because lawlessness will multiply, the love of many will grow cold. But the one who endures to the end will be saved."[ii] Endurance is the mark of a Christ follower. We can persevere because of His power. He is the author and the finisher of our faith. He gives us everything we need to endure. To persist. To stubbornly obey until the end.

MIRACLE MONDAY

That following Monday, James' file was miraculously found and processed. And two Ugandan passports were delivered to my beautiful, air-conditioned hotel room. God did the impossible. Yet again. Our next stop was the US Embassy to apply for our visas. Then the departure gate at Entebbe Airport. The light was beginning to glimmer at the end of my very long tunnel. The sun was beginning to rise. Hallelujah. The end was near.

---

ii   Matthew 24:12-13

chapter 26

Business Class

My last order of business was to set up meetings at the U.S. Embassy to apply for James' and Jolie's visas. Before leaving Texas, we applied for, and were granted, pre-approval to bring two immigrant children back to America. These hearings would allow the government agent to meet all parties involved, go through all our documents with a fine-tooth comb, and ask any relevant questions pertaining to the health and well-being of my babies. Once again, we bussed in Agatha, Issah, and the Muzetati Police Chief to speak on James' behalf, and Ezra from Kisoro to vouch for Jolie's case. Emma and George were also both present. We were quite a party.

The government official who handled our case was a kind woman named Nylah. She thoroughly questioned each individual involved. I was the last person with whom she spoke. Our conversation lasted about 10 minutes, and I was then instructed to return to the Embassy in two days to pick up my babies' visas. We were so close to the end.

GUILTY HAPPINESS

Amidst all our passport drama, Dianna was granted legal guardianship of Job. He was officially her forever family. But much like us, she had run into roadblocks regarding the processing of Job's court documents and passport file. Her time in Uganda had not yet come to an end. She would not be flying home any time soon. I knew that my absence would now leave her alone in a foreign country.

We both cried as I packed up my suitcases, preparing for my journey back to Texas. I had dreamt about going back to the U.S. almost from the moment I arrived in Uganda. God knows how I had ached for my daughters and my husband and my friends and my family. I had been in Uganda for over eight weeks now. I had done the thing. It was finished. I was finally able to leave. I should've been dancing around my hotel room with pure joy. But one look at my miserable friend crushed me. I knew how it felt to be left alone in an unknown land. I knew the feeling of abandonment. I knew that sense of overwhelming grief and fear. There was definitely a part of me that felt guilty for leaving her. But I knew my time in Uganda was over. And so did she.

Thursday morning dawned and found me first in line at the U.S. Embassy. Even though I knew this was our last step before going home and it was a done deal, I still couldn't let myself believe all was well until I had every document in my hands. My experience in Uganda had taught me that seeing was believing. I once again met with Nylah. She handed me two very official sealed manilla envelopes and instructed me to guard them with my life, carry them onto the plane with me, and present them (unopened) to the U.S. Immigration Office when we arrived in

Dallas. These documents were the key to my babies' entrance into the United States of America. I left the U.S. Embassy with two visas and two Ugandan passports in my hands. We were going home.

A generous couple from our church offered to pay for our flights back to Dallas. They had made the journey from Uganda to Texas before and knew exactly what we would need: Business Class seats on Emirates Airlines. They gave us money for two tickets: one for James and one for me with Jolie in my lap. When I arrived back to our hotel from the Embassy, I hopped on my computer and booked our flights for the following day. This was actually happening.

AIN'T NOBODY GOT TIME FOR THAT

That evening, Emma and Sarah hosted a farewell dinner for me at their house. All my friends from Passion Christian Assembly joined us, as well as George, Dianna, and Job. It felt surreal knowing that this would be the last time I'd see most of their faces for a while. These people had become dear to me. Like family. Especially Emma. He was now my brother. I am forever indebted to his kindness and generosity. He had facilitated our adoption every step of the way. Our family was now complete because of him.

While the adults sat around the table enjoying our dinner, the kids were playing noisily around the house. I noticed James had perched himself on the sofa, refusing to join in the fun. I walked over to check on him; he was burning hot with fever. I called Emma over to examine him. It was quickly determined: James was having a malaria flare-up, much like he did the first time we met him in the hospital back in August. I immediately went into panic mode. We were flying home *the next morning*. I literally did not have time for this. Emma retrieved some medicine from a nearby closet and gave James the appropriate dose. "Will I be able to fly home tomorrow?" I desperately asked. "I will examine him again first thing in the morning," was the response I received.

Dianna and I went back to the Sheraton that night with our babies, and I made the final preparations for my 28 hours of travel back to Texas. All my belongings were packed. I had everything I needed for our trip loaded into my carry-on bag, including the sealed envelopes containing the visas. The diaper bag was stuffed with diapers, wipes, multiple changes of baby clothes, snacks, and empty sippy cups. The double-stroller would come in clutch while maneuvering through the airport. I went to bed that night confident everything was in order and I was ready for the long journey.

AIRPORT ADVENTURES

Sleep alluded me. James was sick. The malaria was ravaging his body. He was up most of the night vomiting. I did my best to force him to drink liquids, but to no avail. I knew he would be dehydrated. I knew the situation was bad.

Emma arrived at the hotel first thing the next morning. The bellman had helped me bring all our belongings down to the lobby and we were waiting curbside when Emma pulled around in his SUV. James and Jolie sat sleepily buckled into the stroller.

Dianna and Job had come down to see us off. Her eyes were swollen, giving away the fact she had already spent time crying in her room. My heart broke for her. I hated leaving her there. But my son was sick. And I was convinced the best way to help him was to get him to a hospital in Dallas as soon as possible. I was determined to get on an airplane that day.

We loaded the car with all our belongings and I clung to my friend as she sobbed. I climbed into the back seat with my babies, and we pulled away from the Sheraton. The image of Dianna standing on the hotel curb, holding Job's hand, crying as she watched us drive away will forever be etched in my mind. I uttered a quiet prayer under my breath on her behalf. She would need the God of all comfort in the days to come. I knew He would not fail her.

James was lethargic in my lap, still burning hot to the touch. We got about 10 minutes down the road, and he vomited again. Emma pulled into a medical supply store and came out holding a bag of fluid and an IV needle. He quickly inserted the line into James's arm and hooked the bag of fluid on the back seat passenger handle above the door. He got back behind the wheel and we kept it moving.

"Emma, he's listless," I said, a few minutes later. "He can't keep his eyes open or his head up." Emma then pulled into a parking lot in front of a pharmacy and walked out a few minutes later holding an obscure can. He opened the back door, poured some of the can's contents in his hand, and held it to James's mouth. "This is glucose powder. It will help him gain energy," he instructed me. He handed me the glucose and assumed his position in the driver's seat. I attempted to get the powder in

James's mouth, while avoiding the IV line hanging from the handle above me. He ended up having white powder crusted all around his lips, leaving a striking contrast on his dark skin. It wasn't a good look, but I didn't have time to care. The back seat felt like a medical circus. Emma was speeding down the winding road to the airport. We were running late.

We arrived at the airport an hour later than planned. Emma helped me carry all our trunks and suitcases to the ticket counter. At check-in, I was informed that I would not be able to take the double stroller on the plane. It would need to be checked and I could retrieve it once we landed in Dallas. "No, I need this stroller," I insisted. "I'm traveling 28 hours, including a four-hour layover in Dubai, by myself with two babies. I have to have this stroller." My pleas fell on deaf ears. I was told it was against airline policy to gate-check strollers. My flight had already begun boarding. I didn't have time to sit here and argue. I reluctantly took my babies out of the stroller and handed it to the agent.

I hugged my brother Emma goodbye. He had been my hero in every way imaginable these past nine weeks. Emma had freely given his time, his resources, and his talents to help me accomplish the work God had called me to. He selflessly drove me the entire length of Uganda, through rainstorms, on treacherous mountain roads, safely delivering me to necessary destinations. He provided medical care for my children, he empowered and encouraged me in his local ministry, and he faithfully walked me through the most difficult season of my life. I knew I was forever indebted to Emma. Thankfully, he had plans to visit Texas, so I knew I would see him soon. It helped ease the sting of leaving my brother.

I put Jolie on my hip, stacked the diaper bag on top of my rolling carry-on suitcase, instructed my sick son with a white-powder mouth to grab onto the handle and walk quickly with me. We clumsily made it through security, and I kept my eye on my watch the entire time. We were cutting it close. As we reached our gate, I smelled an all-too familiar scent: Jolie had a blow-out in her diaper. *Dear God in heaven.* I yelled at the gate agent: "We're on this flight! I need to change her diaper real quick. Please don't close the door!" I laid Jolie down on the dirty floor of the Entebbe airport and cleaned her massive diarrhea right there in front of God and everybody. Once she was fresh, I loaded everything back up, handed the agent our tickets, and walked onto the plane. We were the last to board the flight. Business Class was wide open, so I was able to put Jolie in her own seat next to James. I buckled everybody in, handed them some snacks, and settled back in my seat for the eight-hour flight to Dubai. I was sweating profusely.

After takeoff, the flight attendant came around with a meal for each of us. To my relief, James ate almost everything placed in front of him. Jolie ate her fill, too. Once they were both satisfied, I pulled out their little blankies and covered them up. They instantly nodded off and slept for three hours. I also napped like a champ. It had already been a full day. And we were just getting started.

The first leg of our trip went by quickly. James seemed to be feeling a little better, thanks to the IV fluids, glucose powder, and the full meal he'd eaten. We landed in Dubai, and immediately had to go through United Arab Emirates customs. They scanned all three of our passports and ushered us through the line. And there, on the other side of customs, like a glistening ram in the bush, were two baby strollers bearing an Emirates Airlines logo. "Can I use these?!" I desperately asked an airline agent. The approval was given, and I nearly wept with joy. I loaded my babies into the strollers, rigged them together MacGyver-style into a makeshift double stroller using the straps of my diaper bag, and blissfully strolled my way through the Dubai airport. We briefly stopped at the food court for some chicken tenders from Burger King, which James immediately threw up all over the floor, and made our way to the Emirates Airlines Lounge. Lounge access was a perk that accompanied our Business Class tickets, and it was an absolute blessing for our four-hour layover. I found a quiet corner where I could relax in a comfortable chair and let the kids play with their toys. Unlimited food and drinks were offered in the lounge, so I was able to fill up sippy cups with juice and restock the diaper bag with snacks. God knew exactly what we needed. I checked in with Bradley several times before heading to our gate to board the plane that would carry us to Dallas.

We were one 16-hour flight away from being home.

The next airplane we boarded was much larger than our first. Business Class on Emirates was nicer than any First Class seat I had ever experienced. It featured a private pod-like seat that laid out into a bed *with a mattress and pillow*, a personal flat-screen TV, a footrest, and a table for eating. James had his own pod and Jolie would share mine. In God's divine plan, the seat on the other side of mine ended up being the only vacant seat in Business Class on that flight, so Jolie was able to have her own space, as well. We could all spread out and relax. God had paved the way for our flight back to Texas.

About two hours into our flight, James looked at me and said a foreign word I had never heard him utter before. "Paaaahhhhdddddyyyyy." I had absolute zero idea what he was saying and asked him to repeat himself about eight times. It finally hit me. Potty. James wanted to go teetee on the potty. *How incredibly inconvenient.* I had no clue how to go about this. *Do I take Jolie with us? Or do I leave my baby girl in her seat by herself to take my baby boy potty? How does this work?* But God had this figured out, too. About that time, a lovely woman walked over to me and struck up a conversation. She had been watching me with my two babies and wanted to know if she could help me. Her husband was the mayor of Prosper, a suburb north of Dallas, about 20 minutes from our house. We discovered we had several mutual friends and I immediately trusted her. I handed Jolie to her, and marched James to the bathroom, where he sat on the toilet for seven minutes and most definitely did not teetee on the potty. Mrs. Mayor's Wife was my support system for the rest of our 16-hour flight home. God had sent an angel to help me.

I somehow survived that flight home. To this day, I still can't believe I traveled 28 hours around the world by myself with two babies. It sounds insane every time I hear myself say it out loud. The only explanation for my survival is the grace of God. He went before me and met me at every point of need. By the time we landed, I was exhausted in every possible way, but had never been happier to be on American soil. I was back on the same continent as my daughters and my husband. We were in the same time zone. In the same zip code. What a blissful thought. I left for Uganda on August 27, 2012. My plane touched down in Dallas on October 27, 2012. I had officially been away for exactly two months. What I thought would be a three-week experience ended up taking eight weeks and six days. But now my storm was over. I had completed my assignment. God had finished what He started.

We were finally home.

chapter 27

Knight: PARTY OF 7

The International Arrivals terminal at DFW Airport was a party that day. Mrs. Mayor's Wife, the angel that she was, stayed with me until the very end, assisting me with grabbing my luggage, taking my children through U.S. Customs and Immigration, submitting their visas, and hauling everything through the secure double doors where we had about 50 friends and family members eagerly waiting for us with signs, balloons, and flowers. As soon as the doors opened and I saw my daughters, I dropped everything and sprinted toward them, collapsing on the floor under a pile of little girls. I grabbed each of their faces and smothered them with kisses. I was touching them with my own hands.

This wasn't a dream.

Bradley and my parents took James and Jolie out of the stroller and were embracing each of them. All our friends respectfully waited to the side with tears streaming down most of their faces as they observed our family reunion. Ava, Greta, and Harper couldn't hide their delight at meeting their new siblings. James and Jolie were absolute champs during this scene. It wasn't too difficult for me to put myself in their little shoes. I remembered all too well how it felt to be in a foreign country, experiencing new smells, new scenery, new people, new language, new everything. My heart knowingly ached at the culture shock they were silently enduring. So much transition; so much newness. James and Jolie could've easily freaked out at the onslaught of white faces all around them—especially after such a long journey—but they patiently let people come say hi to them, even offering a rare smile to a few lucky friends.

As much as I wanted to sprint out of that airport and get my children to the shelter of our house, I also wanted to honor everyone who came to meet us. I spent time hugging and thanking each person at the airport that day. These were my people. My village. The ones who had shown up for my family through these exhausting nine weeks. They are forever part of my family's story. Our airport party lasted about 45 minutes, and then it was time for the seven of us to go home.

But first, Chick-Fil-A. It was the first American meal James and Jolie ever ate. Because we're good Christians. We filled up on chicken nuggets, waffle fries, and sweet tea, then made our way home. I'll never forget the sight of my extended-length SUV filled to the brim with seven people.

This was our new normal.

Our first few weeks at home were a blessed time with our children. For the most part, we hunkered down at the house, giving everyone time to get to know each other. Our biological daughters and our adopted babies had an immediate connection and instantly loved each other. The girls were eager to share everything in our house: toys, food, blankets, clothes. They played together in our backyard, pushing each other on the swings and showing James and Jolie how to go down the slide.

Halloween was a few days after we got home, so we dressed everyone in costumes and trick-or-treated through the neighborhood. James and Jolie stayed in the wagon while their big sisters collected candy for their treat bags. On the rare occasion that we ventured out for lunch or dinner as a party of seven, it was almost always at a Tex-Mex establishment. Because I'm a good Texan. I needed chips and salsa and fajitas, and my babies needed to learn how to appreciate a good tortilla. After the immensely difficult nine weeks I had just spent in Uganda, those first few weeks easily spent readjusting at home were a gift.

IS THIS ALL A DREAM?

While those initial weeks at home were a blessing with our kids, they were also a dark time for me, personally. I struggled with what I now believe was post-traumatic stress disorder (PTSD). I should have sought counseling and therapy during this time, but unfortunately, I did not. I told you in an earlier chapter that while in Uganda, I would have very vivid dreams about being back in Texas with my girls. I would wake up from those dreams and realize I was still in Africa and launch into a deep depression. When I arrived back in Texas, I still had episodes of panic because I didn't know if I was dreaming or not.

I remember one specific trip to Target. I had Ava and Greta with me to pick up a few items, and in the middle of the $1 section, I had a total meltdown. I began crying and pinching myself, trying to "wake up" because I thought I was dreaming.

Am I really at Target in Dallas? Are my daughters actually here with me? Am I going to wake up soon and be back in Uganda and realize this was all just a dream? My precious girls tried to comfort me the best they knew how. For their sake, I was able to collect myself and push through our shopping trip. When we made it home, I went to our bedroom and sobbed to Bradley. My brain didn't know how to differentiate fiction from reality. The PTSD episodes eventually went away. Day by day, little by little, my brain and my body acclimated to being back in Texas, under the same roof as my husband and all five of my children. The seven of us were all together.

It was an actual dream come true.

STANDING ON HIS PROMISES

On a Wednesday night in late November, I showed up at the end of our church's choir practice with James and Jolie. This group of people had carried me through the entire experience with their prayers. They had loved on our family, provided for us in countless ways, and helped us carry our burdens. The victory of our children's adoption was also their victory. I couldn't wait for them to see the answer to their prayers with their own eyes. When they saw me walk in holding two little Ugandan babies, they stood up and erupted in praise: clapping their hands, screaming, raising their arms in worship. I was given a microphone and led the choir in a new song that had become a pillar of encouragement to me through our entire process:

Can you hear the voice of the Father
Inviting you to walk on the water,
Risk it all, answer the call, and enter in?
Now we stand on every promise.
We're not afraid, our faith goes before us.
When we believe, we're gonna see the
supernatural.
We're gonna see what we're praying for.
We believe every single word.
Stronger than we've ever been,
Standing on his promises.
We're gonna see the impossible.
We release the supernatural.
Stronger than we've ever been,
We are standing on his promises.[15]

I held my children and declared, "You are seeing what you prayed for!" God received a whole lotta glory that night.

THE GOOD DOCTOR

Two days before Thanksgiving, James woke up from a nap, burning hot to the touch. He had that familiar listless look in his eyes, and I knew his malaria was rearing its ugly head again. I took him to the hospital nearest to our house. As soon as we checked into the Emergency Room, I told them, "He has malaria. This is a flare-up." Unfortunately, it took them four hours to test for literally every other disease under the sun before they concurred with my diagnosis. God bless them, they had no idea what to do for a two-year-old with malaria. They were not equipped to handle James' needs, so he was transferred to the nearest Children's Hospital, which had an Infectious Disease Pediatrician on staff who specialized in treating children adopted from other countries. After running a few tests, it was determined James' strand of malaria could be cured and absolutely eradicated after two weeks of oral medication. We would never have to deal with it again. An absolute miracle.

James was discharged on Wednesday afternoon so we could all be home for our first Thanksgiving together. The next day, while the entire family was gathered at our house preparing for our meal, there was a knock on our front door. It was the Infectious Disease Doctor, stopping by to check on James. On Thanksgiving Day. The kindness of this man made me cry. Once again, God knew exactly what we needed and had gone before us. He used the hands and feet of a doctor to show us His love. And we thanked God for all of it. How could we not?

DECEMBER 17, 2012

Dianna came home from Uganda two weeks after I got back. And she came alone. *Without Job.* The passport hold up at Immigration in Kampala was much worse than it had been for me. She was at an absolute standstill with Job's paperwork, so she left him in Emma's care and came home. I was devastated for my friend. I couldn't imagine spending week after week working toward a goal of bringing home your son, only to arrive back in Texas alone. George and Emma were keeping her updated on the passport process, and as soon as it was ready, Dianna's husband Josh would fly to Uganda to bring their son home. We kept praying for this to happen expediently.

December 17, 2012 was a monumental day. Not only was it my 30th birthday, but our tribe appeared before a judge in a United States Courtroom. After being back in Texas for two months, we were able to finalize James' and Jolie's adoption. The cherry on top? Josh arrived at DFW Airport with Job that same day. It was one of the best days of my life.

Our court hearing was prompt, efficient, and joyful. Our judge was a lovely woman who asked many questions about our experience and took the time to greet all five of our children. She was kind and excited about our future as a family of seven. Bradley and I each held a baby in our left hands and raised our right hands as we were sworn in, our daughters standing beside us. James and Jolie were pronounced members of the Knight family and official citizens of the United States of America.

After our appointment with the judge, we loaded our car and drove like crazy to the International Arrivals gate at DFW Airport. My friend was being reunited with her son. Her long journey was coming to an end. I couldn't get there fast enough. A large crowd was gathered at the airport to welcome Josh and Job, who had already come through the double doors and been united with their family. I ran straight to the middle of the chaos and launched myself into Dianna's arms. We held each other and our Ugandan babies and sobbed. We had experiences and memories nobody else would ever understand. We had been delivered through the fire. And now we were all home. We were all together. After months of praying and planning and traveling and crying and working, here we were, side-by-side. Dianna's family of six and my family of seven. A ridiculous circus of 13 people. Trophies of God's confounding grace.

PARTY OF 7

Our family felt complete. We were a tribe of seven—the biblical number for completion. And we were at peace. God did an amazing work of knitting our family together. We witnessed James and Jolie being grafted into our vine in real time. The way all five of our children loved each other and grew together and immediately belonged to one another was nothing short of miraculous. And sitting here, writing this book nine years later, this hasn't changed. Our children fiercely love each other. Do they fight? Duh. They're siblings. But the bond between them is unbreakable.

God has established our family as a solid unit. We all have a seat at the table. We all have a voice to speak our peace. We're thick as thieves. We fight for one another. We cheer each other on. We encourage one another. None of us can get away with tomfoolery because we'll call each other out. We're quick to forgive. We're colorful. We're proud of our differences. We're proud of how God brought us all together. We tend to draw attention everywhere we go. We're a unique group of individuals. We're okay with the attention, because we want to point you to Jesus and all He has done for us. We're large, we're loud, we're crazy, and we own it. We love us.

Thank you, Lord, for our Knight Tribe party of seven.

chapter 28

INSTAGRAM *Ready*

I've known I was supposed to write this book ever since we adopted our babies. I knew God wanted me to tell the story of His faithfulness to our family, and to encourage others to follow Him in stubborn obedience, no matter what. Yet, it took me nine years to finally sit down and write it. I was disobedient to write a book called *Stubborn Obedience*. The irony is not lost on me. Do you want to know why it took me so long? I refused to obey the Lord in the next thing He had for me because I was in pain. I was hurting. I was exhausted.

The two months I spent in Uganda were so difficult and traumatic that when I finally got back to Texas with my babies, I decided I was done with God for a while. I literally said these words out loud: "God, this is too hard for me. Following you has been too painful. I can't do this anymore. Choose somebody else." You won't see this prayer in a tweet any time soon. If you looked on my social media account, everything was great on the outside. I was still serving at my church, still leading worship, still speaking at events, but I was doing it from a place of emptiness.

My well was dry.

It took about two years for the Lord to heal my heart and woo me back to daily communion Him. It took that long for me to realize that being stuck in Uganda for nine weeks was one of the biggest blessings of my life. What I viewed as a setback was actually a setup for deep connection and easier transition with my children. It took time before I could agree with the words of the apostle James:

> Consider it a great joy, my brothers and sisters, whenever you experience various trials, because you know that the testing of your faith produces endurance. And let endurance have its full effect, so that you may be mature and complete, lacking nothing.[i]

My faith was tested and endurance was being produced. It took me a while to be joyful about this. During this season, God never stopped pursuing me, and His love and mercy helped change my perspective on my pain. That which caused me grief ultimately became my greatest gift.

THE REST OF THE STORY

My family of seven looks good on Instagram. My five colorful children are beautiful and always happy. My multiethnic tribe has a cool vibe. My social media feed is a display of cleverly curated images designed to showcase how awesome we are. Our flaws? You won't see them. Our failures? They won't be on a highlight reel anytime soon. Our fights? We never fight.

---

i   James 1:2-4

(Except for when we do.) My Facebook timeline doesn't tell the full story. Our struggles, our trauma, our process isn't there.

Another thing you won't see on social media? The difficult parts of my babies' transition: the night terrors, the emotional shutdowns, the deeply imbedded food insecurities, the bone-chilling fear of animals, the struggles to communicate and openly share feelings. These issues won't get a lot of likes, comments, or shares on Facebook. I don't broadcast this for the world to see. But it's our daily experience. It's easy to see pictures of our happy family and be enamored with the outcome of our labor.

But don't think for a minute it hasn't been difficult.

We've had to fight like crazy for the health of all five of our children. The weapons of our warfare are prayer, counseling, open conversations, empathy, worship, Bible study, and a steady diet of books written by people who are much smarter than us. And God has given us the grace for all of it. It's our honor to be conduits of God's healing and deliverance for our children. This is the very real work of being a parent, adoptive or biological. This is what we are called to do. This is what God gives us the strength to accomplish every day. It's the ongoing ministry of shepherding our tiny flock. And it never ends.

Another thing not heavily featured on my Instagram? Our ongoing dialogue regarding race. Many adoptive parents bring children into their home who share their same race or ethnicity and these conversations are not as urgently necessary. But for our family, there is no dodging the topic or skating around the issue. We have to tackle it head-on. We all look different from one another. James and Jolie have velvety dark skin, Harper and I both tan easily in the summer, and Bradley, Ava, and Greta are all whiter than snow. We all have different hair. James requires a specific barber who can give him a correct fade with sharp edges. Jolie has her hair braided by a beautiful black woman who knows how to help care for her hair. James' and Jolie's skin requires more moisture than mine does. We keep lotion all over the house in an attempt to keep their skin hydrated. Our eyes are different, our noses are different, our lips are different. Instead of trying to minimize or hide our differences, we've decided to embrace and celebrate them. We're proud of how we look! We're proud of our skin and our hair and our lips. We're all made in the image of our Creator. What a colorful God we serve. Instead of striving to be color-blind, we've chosen to live as the color-blessed people of God that we are.

Our diversity is a blessing.

As our kids have grown, we have educated them at an age-appropriate level on the history of racism and slavery in our country. These conversations will no doubt get more and more difficult as they enter their teen years. Bradley and I have made a commitment to educate ourselves and seek counsel from our friends within the black community. We have been intentional to build deep, meaningful relationships with people who do not look like us. We want our children to have godly role models who look like them. As much as I love my daughter, I will never be able to show Jolie how to be a strong, beautiful black woman. The same goes for Bradley and James. We need help with this. We need a diverse village. And God has been remarkably faithful to bring godly, kind, gracious people of color into our world, to do life with, and to help us along the way. Our due diligence and daily commitment to parenting multi-racial children is not something you'll see in an Instagram story or tweet. We're cultivating deep, hidden roots while praying for our well-loved children to bloom into healthy adults.

THE BEGINNING, NOT THE END

The call to adoption didn't end when we brought our babies home in 2012. In fact, that's when the real work began. That's when I discovered stubborn obedience never actually ends—it simply follows the Lord onto the next assignment. Sometimes the assignment is large and highly visible, like adopting children from Africa. Sometimes it's subtle and hidden, like opening your computer and continuing to write your testimony, alone in your bed with no one watching. Both acts of obedience are equally significant because both position God in His rightful place, as Lord of your life. Following God in stubborn obedience is the outward expression of your unwavering belief in His relentless faithfulness.

And that is the point of this entire book.

I asked you several questions in the very first chapter, and I'll ask them again:

- *What has God called you to do?* His calling on your life will most likely be different than ours. It may not be a nebulous task like adoption. You may just be called to walk down the street and deliver a meal to a neighbor in need. Or seek restoration for a broken friendship. Or go back to school. But God has a specific design, plan, and purpose for your life.[ii] He has created you in Christ

---

ii   Jeremiah 29:11

Jesus for good works, which He prepared for you before you were in born.[iii] You were placed on this earth for a reason. What is it, Friend? What has God called you to do?

- *What has God put in you to accomplish that is a million times bigger than you could imagine?* If you have an assignment in front of you that seems easily completed in your own strength, it's most likely not from the Lord. Paul tells us, "But God chose what is foolish in the world to shame the wise; God chose what is weak in the world to shame the strong."[iv] In other words, the whole reason God chose you for this specific assignment is because it's so much bigger than you. It's supposed to be more than you can handle. The Holy Spirit living in you will empower you to accomplish all that God has for you, even if it's a million times bigger than you ever imagined.[v]

- *What dream has God given you that seems impossible?* What do you feel compelled to do, even though you're not qualified, equipped, or prepared? We serve a God who delights in the impossible. We serve a God who calls us *and qualifies us*. We serve a God who chooses to use us *and equips us*. We serve a God who gives vision *and provision*.[vi] To put it bluntly, God is not going to put a divine dream in your heart without bringing it to fruition in your life. He is the author of your faith,

---

iii   Ephesians 2:10
iv   1 Corinthians 1:27 ESV
v   Acts 1:8
vi   Hebrews 13:21

and He is also the finisher of your faith. He completes everything He begins.

Which leads me to my final question:

- *Will you follow God in stubborn obedience?* Will you totally surrender to Him? Will you do the thing He's called you to do? I didn't write this book just so you'd be entertained by my story and think I'm cool. (Although it's totally okay if you think I'm cool.) I wrote this book to declare to you, my dear Friend, that our God is faithful and He will finish what He started in your life. I believe this in the marrow of my bones. I have seen it with my own eyes time and time again. It is a fact of life. You can absolutely trust God.

Stubborn obedience is not easy. Just as I described in my story, you may end up in a foreign land, either literally or spiritually. You may find yourself completely isolated and alone. You may have more questions than you have answers. You may face unbelievable discouragement and intense spiritual warfare. You may grow weary and come to the end of your own strength. You may have people telling you to give up. You may find that your obedience causes those around you to suffer in some way. You may have roadblocks along the journey. You may be pressed on every side.

But will you persevere in stubborn obedience? Will you remain fully surrendered to the One who is eager to prove Himself faithful in your life? My prayer for you is that you will be absolutely convinced of the trustworthiness of God. I pray you will to be strong enough to take Him at His word. I pray you will dare to believe that every word from God is true. I pray you will stand firm on every promise He's given you. I pray you're bold enough to take the next step in front of you. And then the next.

I pray you're vulnerable enough to ask for help when you need it. I pray that you will grow in wisdom and discernment as you accomplish the task set in front of you. I pray you will wield your mighty weapon of worship when confronted by your enemy. I pray you will praise your way to a victory. I pray you will be filled with the Holy Spirit of the living God who will empower you to complete every good work set before you. And I pray you believe in the depths of your stubbornly obedient soul:

He who calls you is faithful; He will surely do it.

Epilogue

You can unbuckle your seatbelt now. Our wild ride has come to an end. How are you feeling? Was the whiplash too intense? Let's go get a massage. Or a manicure. We made it through. I wrote a whole book and you read all of it. These are both major accomplishments.

During the process of writing this book (the very thing I never wanted to do), God gave me instructions as to my next assignment: write another book. And then another one. Friend, the very thing I ran from for years has turned into my newest passion. Writing. Isn't that insane? Our adoption journey is a large story...but it isn't my only story. I have my next 3 books already written in my head.

A lifestyle of stubborn obedience never ends, it simply takes on the form of the next move of God. After the grand experience of adopting from Africa, I was tasked with helping my children heal from their trauma. All 5 of them were marked by the adoption in some way. They all had different needs that required a specific approach. Then we felt the Lord call us away from our home church, which was our entire world, and travel the country while homeschooling our children. (Their teacher was a crazy Mom of 5 who has claimed that she doesn't like kids, so you can imagine how well this turned out.) Then God called us to move our family of 7 to New York City. This move had equally glorious and devastating effects on our kids. After 4 years, it felt like we finally found our groove, and then 2020 happened, and we made the decision to move our family back to Texas. Talk about whiplash? Our children have experienced it.

Our stubborn obedience has caused our family to suffer. Nobody talks about this part. So I'm going to write a book about it. *Is following Jesus worth it? Is my total surrender ruining my kids' lives? Do I trust God enough to believe that this suffering is part of His plan and purpose for their lives? Is He big enough to redeem the pain that my children have endured? Is He really good?* We'll answer these questions together.

So, I guess it's a good thing that we're friends now, because we're going to be spending more time together. I can't wait to meet up with you again in my next book. Bring your coffee. I'll bring my Chick-fil-A tea.

Appendix

I told you in the Introduction that I am not an adoption expert. And this is still very true. But I have such a heart for those who are considering adoption and seeking guidance, wisdom, and answers. I was there. I remember how this feels. So I'm going to do my best to serve you.

This is a very touchy subject and I want to tread carefully here. I debated whether or not to even dive into this discussion. But after much prayer and counsel from friends and members of the adoption community, I am very humbly and graciously presenting this next section to you.

I purposefully left out information about the financial side of adoption in my book. There are several reasons for this. First and foremost, Bradley and I have never discussed the cost of adoption with James and Jolie. To this day, they do not know there was money involved in making them a part of our family. And this has been intentional. We have not ever wanted them to feel as if they were "bought" or "purchased." Their lives are invaluable, priceless, and no human life should ever come with a price tag.

That being said, there is a cost that accompanies adoption.

And sometimes it's okay to talk about it. Financial trepidation is the #1 reason most families don't proceed with adoption. Because it can be an expensive endeavor. Truth be told, Bradley and I didn't have the money to complete 2 international adoptions. But we had such a clear, specific call from God that we trusted Him to provide for us. We truly believed that where God gives vision, He also gives provision. Although I'm definitely not against the idea, we did not participate in any fundraising, simply because we didn't feel led to do it. And God provided for us every step of the way. Every time we needed to make a large withdrawal or pay for a big ticket item, the money was there. No matter how much we needed, the money was miraculously in our account. Through the entire process. It felt similar to the widow with a small jar of oil in 2 Kings 4. She was able to take that little amount and multiply it by faith. She kept pouring until she filled large cisterns full of oil and they overflowed. That was our adoption experience.

I know many families who have held fundraisers as a way to finance their adoption, and give other people the blessing of being a part of their journey. I've seen GoFundMe accounts established, t-shirt sales, bake sales, garage sales, you name it. A quick Google search might help you find organizations in your area that offer grants, matching donations and financial assistance. This is the time to get creative! Invite people into your process. Don't be afraid to ask for help. This is what the family of God is for.

My point is this: don't let a lack of finances be the reason you don't obey the Lord. If God has called you, He will equip you. He has the resources. People are walking around heaven on streets paved with solid gold, for crying out loud. God can afford to help you. And He *will* help you. But you must first obey.

Below you will find a short list of adoption resources. I hope you find these helpful!

BOOKS:
- The Connected Child; Karen Purvis
- Created to Connect; Karen Purvis
- The Whole-Brained Child; Daniel J. Siegel
- The Wounded Heart; Dan Allendar
- Before You Were Mine; Susan TeBos

WEBSITES:
- www.empoweredtoconnect.org
- www.showhope.org
- www.howtoadopt.org
- www.child.tcu.edu
- www.puregiftofgod.org

SOCIAL MEDIA ACCOUNTS:
- @empoweredtoconnect
- @therapyredeemed
- @bethebridge
- @adoptwell
- @thearchibaldproject

And lastly, but certainly nowhere near the least; I cannot let you close this book without giving you the opportunity to support my dear brother Kasadha Emma and the work he's doing in Uganda. Since our adoption in 2012, Emma has gone on to receive his medical doctorate, start a private Christian school, and launch a child sponsorship program. The babies who have been born in his clinic now have an opportunity to go to school and receive an excellent education. Emma is literally changing the country of Uganda for the glory of God. You can learn more about his ministries and support him financially through his stateside ministry partner, Engage Hope.

(https://www.engagehope.org/ministry-partners/passion-christian-ministries)

Acknowledgments

Bradley – No one believes in me, cheers for me, or encourages me more than you. You are my rock, my compass, my anchor, my mirror, my partner, my covering, my best friend. Thank you for opening doors for me and for pushing me into my calling. I love you with all of my heart.

Ava, Greta, Harper, James, and Jolie – Thank you for letting me tell our story. Thank you for being patient with me during the many nights I stayed up late to write. Thank you for encouraging me. Thank you for cheering for me. Thank you for being proud of me. The 5 of you are my reason for everything I do. I love you with all of my heart.

Mom – Thank you for leading me to Uganda. Thank you for stepping in while we were away and taking care of my girls, building bunk beds, decorating rooms, and keeping everyone alive. Thank you for teaching me how to serve others by your example. I love you.

Janie – Remember that time you stayed with my 3 girls while I was in Uganda and you said it was the hardest thing you'd ever done in your life? And now you have 4 children under the age of 5 and own 7 restaurants. (Shout out to The

Biscuit Bar.) I feel like I deserve some credit for preparing you for all of this. So…you're welcome? (Also thank you. You're my best friend forever.)

Dianna – I still can't believe we did it. And we did it together. Only God could come up with such a ridiculous, redemptive plan. Thank you for being with me and for me all of these years. Our 9 kids are all big now. We used to get asked if we ran a daycare center when they were little. We don't get asked that question anymore. How sad. Also thank you for being my neighbor. I love that our families get to do life together. I love you.

Lisa – What a humongous journey we've been on together. You were there at the very beginning and have stood in as a surrogate mother/grandmother on countless occasions. You've counseled me, mentored me, and loved me unconditionally. I am forever grateful for you.

Angie – You are the Great Connector. You have been invested in my story from the start. You cared about our adoption, and you cared about this book. You introduced me to Stacey, and were my sounding board throughout the entire process. Thank you for your wisdom. Thank you for your friendship. Thank you for writing my foreword. Everybody needs an Angie in their life.

Stacey – The Lord brought you into my life. Good grief, He is so good to me. You were exactly who I needed to help me put my thoughts in order and on paper. You are an incredible coach and cheerleader, and an even better friend. This is just the beginning for us.

Becky – Our book-writing timelines ran parallel to one another's. I believe God gave us each other for this season to encourage each other and cheer one another on. Thank you for the time you invested in me to help me finish this project. (P.S. Everybody go buy her book *The Pivot* ASAP.)

Debbie, Becky, Lisa, Tasha, Angie – My fabulous Focus Group. You all took your *extremely valuable* time to carefully read through my manuscript and give me your priceless feedback on my writing. You are all experts in your fields of ministry and I do not take for granted the fact that you believed in me enough to offer your wisdom and support. I am grateful for each one of you.

Dara – Thank you for holding my hand through my entire adoption process. You were patient with me and incredibly kind to me. I love that our Ugandan girls are BFF's. Abigail and Jolie are a force!

Tina – Thank you for being willing to take my call and point me in the right direction with this book. Thank you for speaking truth to me: "Be obedient and start writing. God will bring the right people into your life to help you." This turned out to be profoundly true. I'm thankful for you.

Kasadha Emma – I saved you for last. I don't even know how to begin to say thank you. Our family would not be complete if it weren't for you. You worked tirelessly to help us complete our adoption. The hours and hours (*and hours*) in the car driving across Uganda, the court dates, the meals, the prayers, the tears, the agony, the laughter, the joy…you were there for it all. You are a giant in the kingdom of God, and I get to call you my brother. I love you and Sarah and your children so very deeply. I pray that God continues to bless you as you bless your country. I am eternally grateful for you.

Endnotes

1   Batterson, Mark. *The Circle Maker.* Zondervan, 2011.

2   Jason Ingram, Matt Redman, and Tim Wanstall. *"Never Once."* sixsteprecords/Sparrow Records, 2011.

3   https://en.wikipedia.org/wiki/Polygamy_in_Uganda

4   https://www.trade.gov/country-commercial-guides/uganda-agricultural-sector

5   https://caritas.us/blog/ugandan-surnames-understanding-whats-in-a-name

6   https://blog.compassion.com/author/chrisgiovagnoni/

7   https://utmost.org/what-my-obedience-to-god-costs-other-people/

8   Jackie Gouche Farris. *"My Help Cometh from the Lord."* Brooklyn Tabernacle Music, 1999.

9   TerKeurst, Lysa. *Uninvited.* Thomas Nelson, 2016

10   Richard Smallwood. *"I'll Trust You."* Zomba Recording, 2006.

11   https://www.merriam-webster.com/dictionary/mercy

12   https://www.biblestudytools.com/lexicons/greek/nas/ekklesia.html

13   Chris Tomlin, Matt Redman, Matt Maher, Jason Ingram. *"White Flag."* sixsteprecords/Sparrow Records, 2012.

14   https://www.merriam-webster.com/dictionary/sin

15   David Binion, Joshua Dufrene, William McDowell. *"Standing."* Integrity Music, 2012.

Made in the USA
Monee, IL
07 July 2022